Extract from Regimental History of 69th Punjabis.

During the 1st Burmese War, 1824-26, for the gallantry displayed by all ranks in spite of sickness and hardship during the AVA Expedition and in consideration of "the readiness always evinced" by the Regiment to proceed on Field Service (up to the 1st Burmese War in 1824 the Regiment had served overseas eight times a number unattained by any other Indian Regiment), it was granted the badge of a Galley with motto "KHUSHKI-O-TARI" (G.O. No. 121 of 1839).

This reward took the shape of the badge and motto, the battalion having been the first Indian Regiment to volunteer to cross the sea for service, (1796) in spite of the fact that by so doing the sepoys concerned broke their caste. During this campaign, they were present at the taking of the Island of AMBOYNA, and the capture of Colombo in Ceylon.

HISTORY OF THE 1ST BATTALION,

2ND PUNJAB REGIMENT

LATE, 67TH PUNJABIS:, AND ORIGINALLY,

7TH MADRAS INFANTRY

1761 - 1928

COMPILED BY

COLONEL N. OGLE, D.S.O.,

and

LIEUT: COLONEL H. W. JOHNSTON

(BOTH, AT ONE TIME, OFFICERS OF THE BATTALION)

The Naval & Military Press Ltd

Published by
The Naval & Military Press Ltd
5 Riverside, Brambleside, Bellbrook
Industrial Estate, Uckfield, East Sussex,
TN22 1QQ England

Tel: +44 (0) 1825 749494

Fax: +44 (0) 1825 765701

www.naval-military-press.com

www.military-genealogy.com

In reprinting in facsimile from the original, any imperfections are inevitably reproduced and the quality may fall short of modern type and cartographic standards.

C O N T E N T S

Page

Chapter I	The Army in India, and it's Evolution.	1
Chapter II	The 7th Madras Infantry.	8
Chapter III	Reports. Crimes, and Punishments.	21
Chapter IV	The New 7th Madras Infantry (67th Punjabis)	26
Chapter V	The Great War. Mesopotamia.	33
Chapter VI	The Great War. Mesopotamia. Operations at Nasiriyeh.	40
Chapter VII	The Great War. Kut-El-Amara.	45
Chapter VIII	Mesopotamia and elsewhere.	53
Chapter IX	Back in India.	66
Chapter X	The 2/67th Punjabis.	69
Appendix "A"	Badges and Devices.	72
Appendix "B"	Battle Honours.	77
Appendix "C"	List of Commandants.	79
Appendix "D"	Roll of British Officers 1902-1928.	80
Appendix "E"	Roll of Officers attached during the Great War.	81
Appendix "F"	Honours and Awards 1915 - 1920.	82
Appendix "G"	Letter of Commendation.	86

CORRIGENDA

P.8.	L.35	For 1774	read	1744
P.16.	L.7	" Kuarnool	"	Kurnool
P.26.	L.7	" Mozbis	"	Mazbis
P.31.	L.38	" areas	"	arms
P.47.	L.34	" Muredin	"	Nuredin
P.52.	L.16	" O.B.S.	"	O.B.E
P.75.	L.1	" reinstituted	"	reconstituted

CHAPTER I

THE ARMY IN INDIA, AND IT'S EVOLUTION

In tracing the history of a Battalion of the Indian Army, which goes as far back as the old 7th Madras Infantry, one must carry out research to the reasons which called for the inception of the Army in India. It is a mistake to look upon India as a portion of the Empire that was conquered by the British: such is not the case - the evolution of the Army in India was brought about by contributory causes which were in no way based upon a policy of conquest. It must be realised, that, with the exception of the basis on which the Indian Defence Force was placed, during the Great War, the Army in India has been, throughout, a voluntary force. There seem to have been five distinct main periods, into which a retrospect of this process of evolution may be divided:-

- A. 1600 - 1708 A.D. During this period the forces of the East India Company were unorganised and isolated units.

- B. 1709 - 1857 A.D. The time of the Presidency Armies, under the East India Company.

- C. 1858 - 1894 A.D. The Presidency Armies continuing, but no longer under the East India Company - under the British Crown.

- D. 1895 - 1920 A.D. The period of union, which followed the abolition of the Presidency Armies.

- E. 1921 - A.D. - onwards: The period of consolidation, coupled with further organization.

There is so much of interest in these different periods, that it may repay one to look briefly at their outstanding features in turn.

A. In December 1600, a charter was granted by Queen Elizabeth, to a commercial association, which called itself "The Company of Merchants of London trading unto the East Indies". A few years later, in 1613, this Company was given the permission of the Mogul Emperor, to establish a factory in Surat. This was the origin of the Bombay Presidency. In 1625 a centre was formed at Masulipatam, and later it was moved to Armegaon, on the same coast. In 1640 the concession of Madras was granted, and this formed the first independent position of the British in India. The concession included the building of Fort St. George, and in this way originated the Presidency of Madras.

In 1634 Emperor Shah Jehan permitted the Company to establish factories in Bengal, and a fort at Piplee. In this was the foundation of the Bengal Presidency. In every case the factories thus founded, had to be provided with guards: and to fulfil this duty, the method of enrolment was followed, the enrolled personnel consisting of ill-disciplined Europeans, and ill-armed native peons. These can scarcely be looked upon as soldiers, but were intended to fill the role of chowkidars. The earliest force that can be considered to have been the germ of the Army in India, originated in Bombay. In 1662, the Island of Bombay was ceded by the Crown of Portugal, to King Charles II, as a portion of the Queen's marriage settlement, and a detachment of King's troops, supplemented by local enrolments, formed it's garrison. But this arrangement did not long continue. The cost of upkeep was a thorn in the regal side; in addition a certain amount of trouble was caused by the ill-feeling that prevailed between the Governor, and the representative of the Company. This led to the offer, by the King, of the Island of Bombay to the Company, on a yearly rental of £10 in gold. This offer was made and accepted in 1668, and at the same time the King's troops were offered service under the new masters. In this deal the King's troops were transferred from King to Company. The pendulum swung the other way 190 years later, when, after the Mutiny in 1857, the Company's European troops were transferred to Crown Service. The Company found it advisable, as years passed, to inaugurate various changes and modifications, but it was not until 1696 that an important change took place. In that year the Company's agent succeeded in gaining permission to fortify his factory at Chattanuttee, and Fort William was then constructed. This remained, for 200 years, the Headquarters of the Army in India.

In 1698, a new Company also received a charter from England, and these two Companies amalgamated, their full name being "The United Company of Merchants of England, trading to the East Indies".

They were usually, and historically known as the East India Company. This Company immediately undertook the formation of the three Presidencies; each one was quite distinct from the others, and was circumscribed by it's own limits. In this way the Presidency Armies followed suit, and the Presidency Army system was established. At that time the Army in India was composed of various types: there were Europeans recruited from England, or locally collected; half caste Goanese Topasses; and Indian sepoys. The last used their own weapons, wore their usual dress, and had their own Native Officers.

B. Although the forces employed were intended only for protective purposes, the numbers gradually increased, and in 1741, we find the first record of a regular Battalion being used in the garrisoning of the Castle in Bombay. Seven years later a form of organised artillery was introduced, and in the same year, Major Lawrence, "the father of the Indian Army" was appointed Commander-in-Chief of all the Company's forces in India, with his Headquarters at Fort St. David 100 miles N. of Madras and 12 miles S. of the French town of Pondicherry. The war with France, which ended in 1748, had tended to bring about a substantial increase in the enrolment of Indian troops, since neither country involved in the war could afford to send out regular troops to India. On the further outbreak of war in 1754, the first Royal troops arrived as reinforcements in Madras. Among these was included the 39th Foot (1st Bn. the Dorsetshire Regt.) which adopted, at a later date, the title of "Primus in Indis".

In 1757 the reorganisation of the Indian troops into regular Battalions was undertaken by Clive, and in each Battalion was a small nucleus of British officers. The composition was 3 B.Os., several British Sergeants, 42 Indian officers, and 820 Indian Rank and File. It is interesting to note that, while introducing British elements the previous Indian officers still remained: there was still an Indian commandant, under the British Captain, and the proportion of Indian to British officers was high. Of this old system the only survival of British N.C.Os. in an Indian unit, is found with the Sappers and Miners.

After the battle of Plassey in 1758, the territories of the Company expanded, and with them, the numbers of troops maintained: and these factors lead to a further reorganisation becoming necessary. This was started in 1796, by which year the Indian troops reached a figure of 57,000. The reorganisation was naturally slow, and was not concluded till 1804, but among the various measures taken, was the first renumbering of units. Further, cavalry and infantry officers, who had hitherto been placed on one general list for the purposes of promotion, were now placed on separate lists. Furlough and pension rules were framed, and an establishment instituted for General officers. In the scope of this brief retrospect, it is not feasible to enter into full details as regards numbers, etc, but it is worthy of record that each Indian Infantry Battalion was given 22 British officers - nearly the same as a unit of the Imperial Forces. This naturally brought in its train a decrease in the status and authority of the Indian officers. Between 1797 and 1857, the further expansion of the Company's territories involved the expansion of the spheres of activity of the Presidency armies. This finally brought about not only the abolition of those armies, but also the necessity for raising irregular corps, and local contingents, to meet extended requirements. Further reorganisation was found necessary in 1824, when units were renumbered according to their Presidencies. Many grave difficulties arose over the question of the employment of troops from one or other of the Presidencies, for the occupation of newly acquired territories, and much discontent prevailed. Mutinies were not unknown, and this spirit of unrest, aided by the dearth of good land communications, by the efforts of revolutionaries, and by the use of seditious propaganda, was partly responsible for the outbreak in 1857. In order to meet the needs of garrisoning the newly acquired territories, resort was made, as already shown, to the raising of local bodies of troops, for particular service, in particular localities. Of these, the most notable were the Hyderabad Contingent, and the Punjab Irregular Force, which became later the Punjab Frontier Force.

C. On November 1st 1858, by Royal Proclamation, Queen Victoria assumed the direct government of India, and the East India Company practically ceased to exist. The Company's European Infantry became British Regiments of the Line, and the Bengal, Madras, and Bombay Artillery were amalgamated with the Royal Artillery. The Indian troops were once more reorganised, beginning in 1861, and the three Presidency Staff Corps were formed, for the purpose of providing British officers for the Indian units. Each Staff Corps was placed on a separate seniority list. In 1877 Her Majesty the Queen assumed the title of Empress of India. Between 1879 and 1891 the seeds were sown which bore fruit in the union of the Presidency armies, and the Military Accounts and Ordnance Departments were united. In 1886-7 the system of linked Battalions came into being, under which the 7th M.I. was linked with the 9th and the 14th. At the same time a Reserve for the Indian armies was formed. In 1891 the three Presidency Staff Corps were united in one Indian Staff Corps.

D. From April 1st 1895, the Presidency Armies were abolished, and the Army in India was divided into 4 Commands: Punjab, Madras, Bengal, and Bombay. In addition, certain local corps already in existence were under the control of the Government of India direct, - such as the Hyderabad Contingent, the Central India Horse, the Bhopal Battalion, the Meywar Bhil Corps, and others. It should be borne in mind, that although the new organisation brought all the forces directly under the Commander-in-Chief, these Commands were as separate from each other as the old Presidencies' had been, and the unification of the Army in India was by no means yet complete. In November 1902, Lord Kitchener took up the appointment of Commander-in-Chief in India, and at once commenced the reorganisation and redistribution of the Army in India. As the 7th Madras Infantry was one of the many battalions whose entity was completely changed under this scheme, and as the results to the Army in India and the changes then introduced, were very far-reaching, it is considered desirable to enter into these changes in some detail.

1. In January 1903, the title "Indian Staff Corps" was abolished, and the officers belonging to that corps were designated "Officers of the Indian Army". The officers, as well as the rank and file of Indian units, belonged to "The Indian Army".

2. Burma was separated from Madras, and became the Burma Command.

3. The Hyderabad Contingent was broken up, and delocalised.

4. The Punjab Frontier Force, with the Frontier District, was distributed between the Peshawar, Kohat, and Derajat Districts.

5. All units of the Indian Army were renumbered in sequence, according to their arms (with the exception of the Gurkha Battalions) and mention of the designations of the old Presidency Armies was omitted.

These measures alone, were almost sufficient to complete the unification of the Indian Army, but there were further measures introduced. The following principles were inaugurated:-

(i) The main function of the Army was to meet aggression from the North West Frontier.

(ii) The army, in peace, to be organised, distributed, and trained, in units of command, as for the field in War.

(iii) Internal security measures were to be the means of freeing the Field Army to carry out it's duties.

(iv) All fighting units, in their several spheres, to be capable of carrying out all the roles of an Army in the Field, and to have equal chances, in experience and training, for bearing those roles.

The central feature of the original scheme was to divide the Army in India (exclusive of Aden, Burma, Chitral, Kohat, and Derajat) into 3 Army Corps (Northern, Western and Eastern) of 3 Divisions each. In 1904 the Secretary of State for India sanctioned the carrying out of the scheme, as far as could be done without involving extra expenditure, and the 9 Divisions were thus established. The Madras Command, as being superfluous to the scheme, was abolished. It could not be expected that experience would not prove that improvement was desirable later, and in 1908 the Army was divided into 2 Armies only, the Northern and the Southern.

The redistribution, as recommended by Lord Kitchener, had not been finally completed at the outbreak of the Great War in 1914, but it was due to the following out of his principles that the Army in India was enabled to take up it's share in the struggle, as promptly as it did. To this may be added, as proof, the fact that on August 1st 1914, the total strength of the fighting services of the Indian Army, of all ranks, was 155,423. By the time the Armistice came, this number had risen to 573, 484.

E. The discovery of certain defects in the system, which were realised during the Great War, called for a further reorganisation, which was started in 1921. A reference to a current Indian Army List, will show the allocation of the present Commands, Districts, &c, and these need not be detailed here, but certain outstanding changes are worth noting. In 1922 the Regimental system was introduced into the Indian Infantry (excluding Gurkhas) and the Battalions composing each Regiment, have a mutual bond of interest in the Training Battalion. To this each Battalion provides a certain number of personnel, and it is on this Training Battalion that each of the remaining Battalions of the Regiment is ultimately dependent for efficiency. Cavalry Regiments became linked in groups, The 4 command system came into use in 1921, and the distribution of troops was arranged according to the principle that the striking force must be fully ready to function, in the case of War. To ensure this, the Army in India was divided into three categories of troops:-
    1. Covering Force.
    2. Field Army.
    3. Internal Security Troops.
It will not be out of place to mention here, one of the most momentous decisions brought about by the Great War, as far as the Indian Army is concerned. That was, to render Indians eligible to hold the King's Commission. This step was partly a natural consequence of the throwing open of high appointments in the civil branches of administration, to Indians; generally, to India's political evolution; and, further, as a just recognition of the loyalty and gallantry displayed by all ranks of the Indian Army during the Great War. In 1924, the Commander-in-Chief announced the decision to Indianize eight regular units. These consisted of 2 Cavalry, 1 Pioneer, and 5 Infantry. The period within which a unit can be completely Indianized in its establishment of officers, is determined, primarily, by the time it takes for an officer in the normal course, to reach the height of commanding a battalion. For this reason alone, the experiment is still in its earliest stages, at this moment, and it's future success, or otherwise, cannot be foreseen. But the significance of the move, and the wide extent of it's implications, are self-evident.

CHAPTER II

THE 7TH MADRAS INFANTRY

In order to follow the narrative of the 7th Madras Infantry, as one of the units of the Army, it is necessary to revert for a brief glance to the Madras Army. As has been recorded, Madras was founded in 1639. Its first main stronghold was Fort St.George, which came into being in 1644, but it's Military History did not begin until a century later. During that time, the settlement - a trade settlement only - was compelled to employ certain of its people in fighting outside their normal business. But this was not war. The East India Company carried arms for its own protection only, and made use of them purely against raid and attack. But it must be remembered that the Company did not engage in fighting for the sake of fighting: on the contrary, as soon as they realised that the act of fighting had a deleterious effect on trade, they did all in their power to avoid it. And when the fighting became a necessity, the Company were careful to arrange that such action should be taken only on their responsibility, and under their supervision. For instance, in 1686, when the Company used an expedition against the Great Moghul Aurunzebe, troops were sent from England to their assistance. But it was ordered that these troops should be sent out under the command of subalterns only: the Company were anxious that the Captains, and senior officers should be found from their own Civil servants in India. This particular expedition, it may be noted, failed, on account of the want of discipline among the troops employed. One can imagine what the feeling would be if a similar method was authorised in officering troops for war in the present day! The Company, however, were centred essentially on trading, and did not recognise any necessity for the formation and upkeep of a standing army. This is shown by their failure to take any recognised steps to protect themselves against attack from Pondicherry in 1774, when war broke out between England and France. The result was that Madras capitulated on the first attack made against it in 1746. In consequence of this, the Government of the Coast of Coromandel devolved upon the Governor and Council in the old Fort St.David, who immediately began to raise troops: and that movement was systematically carried on afterwards. The troops so raised included European Cavalry, Artillery, and Infantry, and Native Infantry. As the history of the

7th Madras Infantry deals only with that portion of the forces so raised, and maintained. Mention will not be made here of the European troops, in detail. Interested readers are referred to the many records available, for information and study on that head.

The history of the Madras Sepoy was not attempted for many years, the first to be published being by Lt.Col: W.J.Wilson, who published his most interesting and valuable work in Madras in 1882. The Madras Army was called, originally, the Coast Army, and their services date, as already noted, from 1746. Between that year, and the first effort at compiling a history, early records had accumulated to such an extent, that an order was made for their reduction. In giving effect to this order much material that would have been of the greatest use in compiling the history, was destroyed; but sufficient remained to make a reasonably accurate account of the various steps forward. The first Sepoy levies were not only undisciplined, but were without any inherent idea that such a factor as discipline was in any way necessary. Their weapons were of all sorts and kinds, varying from bows and arrows to matchlocks, the levies themselves were of different strengths, each under it's own chief. The chief received, from the Government, the pay of the whole body, and he was supposed to distribute this pay. The pay was regularly issued to these chiefs, but it seems to be doubtful whether any measures were taken to ensure it's correct distribution: whatever may have happened, however, the recipients apparently considered their pay, as received, to be sufficiently good to render dismissal from the service a very real punishment. In reviewing the later records of the Madras Army, with it's many glories and honours, it is difficult to understand how the Madras Government could have maintained, (as they did till 1758) such a poor opinion of the natives of the Carnatic. It is all the more surprising considering that they had, before their very eyes, the example of the French, who had trained their sepoys, drawn from the same district, from a much earlier period, with excellent results. In 1758, however, the hands of the Madras Government were forced to use the Carnatic by two main factors, the absence of most of their own troops on service in Bengal, and the prospect of another war with France. In spite of the Government's apparent indifference, during that period, improvements had nevertheless been made. Generally, European N.C.Os. were sent with two or more Native parties; muskets came to replace matchlocks, and an idea of drill was acquired by men serving alongside European troops. In 1758 the Government were unable to meet the French in the field, and Fort St. George fell: this was followed by an advance against Madras itself. This caused the Government to set about the task of "putting it's house in order" and the first two Battalions of Sepoys are referred to in a return of December 1758. In subsequent years, others were raised, until, in November 1765, the establishment was fixed at 10 Battalions. This was increased as time went on.

It will be easier to use the more generally known titles of the Battalion throughout this History, namely the 7th Madras Infantry, the 67th Punjabis, and the 1/2nd Punjab Regiment, according to the title which was correct at any given time.

The actual changes in nomenclature are as follows:- The "Cooke-ki-Pultan" was raised at Trichinopoly in 1761 as the 8th Battalion of Coast Sepoys. Became the 8th Carnatic Battalion 1769; the 7th Carnatic Battalion 1770; the 7th Madras Battalion 1784; the 1st Battalion, 7th Regiment of Madras Native Infantry 1796; the 7th Regiment of Madras Native Infantry 1824; the 7th Regiment of Madras Infantry 1885; the 7th Madras Infantry 1901; 67th Punjabis 1903; and the 1st Battalion 2nd Punjab Regiment 1922. The first record of its use, is in the year of it's raising, when it formed part of the force under Col: Caillaud, in operations against Vellore, in order to force the Rajah of Tanjore to pay the arrears due by him to the Nawab of the Carnatic, as a part of the money required to meet the expenses of the war which resulted in the conquest of the French settlements in April, 1761. Records of further actions in 1762 are meagre, and the location of the Battalion does not appear to be traceable accurately. Existing old Regimental records give the station, between 1760 and 1764, as Poolicat, but this is not corroborated by research. One authority states that, in 1762, when the expedition against Manilla was sent after war had been declared with Spain, the Battalion was included in the order for garrison troops at Vellore. But it appears certain, that between 1764 and 1767, the Battalion formed part of the force employed, under Col: Campbell, against the Polygar chiefs, of the Centre and South Carnatic. These chiefs were, for the time, reduced to submission.

When the Madras Army was reorganised in 1765, the establishment of Native Infantry was fixed at 10 Battalions of 10 Companies each, (two of these being

Grenadier Companies), each Battalion having a Commandant, who was also Subadar of one of the Companies. Each Company was 100 strong, (including 2 Tom-toms, 1 Vakeel, and 1 Packall). For the care of each Battalion were appointed one Captain, two Subalterns, and five Sergeants-Major, in addition to the "black Commandant" (as he was designated in the Military Regulation authorising the establishment). An extract from the wording of the Sepoy's oath on parade, is interesting:- "I do also faithfully promise and swear, that whenever I have an inclination to quit the service, I will give a month's notice of it to my Commanding Officer".

At the same time, the Governor and Council instituted Warrants or Commissions, for all Commandants, Subadars, and Jemadars, which only could be forfeited by their (the Council's) express orders, or by the sentence of a Court Martial. The same document makes reference to the way that "black Sepoy Officers" often show themselves to be remiss in the matter of good order and discipline, and exhorts the European officers to strive to instil these attributes, and to realise that "this Service is regarded as equally honourable, and essential, with the command of Europeans".

In 1767, the Battalion formed part of Col: Smith's force at the battle of Chengamah, on Sept: 2nd, against a portion of Hyder Ali's forces, and this is the first mention of the C.O. of the Battalion being Captain Cooke. In the Indian Army Lists of date before the grouping system came into force, the 67th Punjabis (late 7th Madras Infantry) were also shown as Cooke-Ki-pultan. Although the name of the first C.O. is spelt sometimes without, and sometimes with, the final "E", it may be accepted that the Army List spelling is correct. In Col: Smith's report on the operations, he refers to Capt. Cooke's Grenadiers having distinguished themselves greatly. From the same report, it appears that the sepoys, at this period, were destitute of medical aid, as he says, "I wish the hospital was amply provided with surgeons. We could then afford some succour to the poor and brave sepoy who is wounded and loses a limb in the service". The Battallion also took part in the battle of Trenomally on the 26th September. In his report on this engagement, Col: Smith uses a phrase which might well have been retained in official despatches:- "It is now my duty, and my happiness to pay a just tribute to merit...", and this includes the 7th Madras Infantry. The troops then returned "to Cantonments" but the actual station of the Battalion is doubtful. Again, with Col: Smith's force, the Battalion took part, in 1768, in the siege of Tingerycottah, and other minor actions. Again, in 1769, with the same force, they were engaged at Chittapet, and when, on April 3rd, Hyder Ali was about to sign the treaty of peace, and heard that Col: Smith's force was in the vicinity, only 12 miles away, he insisted on the force being withdrawn to a distance of 25 miles, until affairs could be finally settled. The 7th was once more on service in 1771, against the Rajah of Tanjore, and later, in April 1772, against the Polygars of Madura, and Tinnevelly. The Battalion was then stationed at Trichinopoly. In this same year, an order was issued that all sepoys should wear blue facings, turbands, and cummerbunds, and that the drawers should be bordered with blue. It was in the same year, also, that the practice of inflicting corporal punishment without trial was prohibited, and officers were required to understand "the Moorish language, which is the general language of Hindoostan." In August, the Battalions were formed into Brigades, the 7th being one Battalion in the 1st Brigade, which consisted of 6 Battalions; and the European Officers were fixed at 1 Captain, 5 Subalterns, and 5 Ensigns, for each Battalion. Another contemporary change took the form of a certain stress being laid on the necessity for an allowance of practice ammunition for musketry purposes. Although the Battalion does not appear as a whole in the second taking of Pondicherry in 1778, its Grenadier companies took part in the action, the force being commanded by Maj: Gen: Hector Munro.

In July 1780 Hyder Ali invaded the Carnatic, and the Battalion was engaged in the actions undertaken by Col: Baillie's force during that month, towards Conjeveram. This operation was a failure, due to lack of reconnaissance, and, in spite of assistance being sent, the force had to retreat to Madras. The Regimental records show the Battalion as having been present at the capture of Negapatam in 1779; but this actually took place in 1781, and works consulted do not bear out it's presence on that occasion, so it would appear to be an error. In 1782, the Battalion formed a part of the 2nd Brigade of Col: Fullarton's force against Coimbatore and Seringapatam, the C.O. being Lt: Col: Mackenzie. At the end of that year, Hyder Ali died from a carbuncle, and Tippoo became the head of the enemy's forces; but he signed a peace treaty in 1784. A curious state of affairs is shown by records, of this period. There was grave discontent in the Army, caused by the men's pay being held in arrears, and it is to be noted that these arrears were not fully paid up until 1789. This refers only to the Native troops, and it is stated that "the Native Army, serving alien masters, was kept constantly in arrears for several consecutive years, notwithstanding which, and the extreme severity of the service, it steadily resisted, with few exceptions, the numerous offers conveyed by the emissaries of Hyder and Tippoo. Such fidelity, under similar circumstances is without parallel in the military history of any nation". If the historian had possessed a prophetic insight, he would have been enabled to foresee the similar lack of result to be achieved by the Turks, in their efforts to seduce the loyalty of the Indian Army in the Great War nearly a century and a half later.

In 1780 the order was first published, which made the promotion of Sepoy officers be by seniority. As regards the troops, this extract from Col: Fullarton's report at the beginning of 1784, is of interest:- "The troops have carried their provisions on their backs from Palghautcherry to Dindigul, and have enough remaining to subsist them as far as Madura, being nearly 200 miles. I mention this circumstance........as a proof of the willing spirit of your sepoys in this quarter, who have borne all their hardships with alacrity seldom equalled, and never surpassed." A fine groundwork for the young Madras Army, and the future Indian Army.

In March 1789, the Battalion was again on service, under Col: Stuart against Fort Callangoody. At this time there was in existence a curious rank, subsequently cancelled, that of Captain-Lieutenant! Up to 1784 there had been a difference between the "Circar" and "Carnatic" Battalions: those serving in the North were called "Circar" Battalions, and, later, became the "Madras" Battalions: those serving in the south numbering 1 to 13, were called the "Carnatic" Battalions. This difference was abolished, and in 1784 and 1785 all battalions became known as Madras Battalions. In 1785 the Native Commandant was abolished also. This was brought about by the sentence passed on the Native Commandant of one Madras Battalion (not the 7th), on a charge of "exciting his men to mutiny" to be blown from the mouth of a gun. In the order from the C-in-C, abolishing the rank of Native Commandant, he stated, "When they are clever men, their influence over the Native Officers and Sepoys becomes dangerous: and when they are not so, they can be of no use." The logical reasoning appears irrefutable! But the results of the fidelity of the troops led to the General Order authorising, on behalf of the Government, a medal, with an inscription of the word "Fidelity". The medal was to be of gold for commissioned officers, and of silver for N.C.Os, and men. But, unfortunately, it does not appear that these medals were ever issued.

In 1786 the native troops were formed into Brigades, the 7th being part of the 1st Brigade, and stationed somewhere in the Trichinopoly district. In 1790, war again broke out with Tippoo, and the Battalion was in the 2nd Bde: (Lt: Col: Trent) in General Medow's force, in the operations against Coimbatore, and Dindigul. On the junction of Gen: Medow's force with that of Col: Maxwell at Poolanhully, the Brigades were changed, and the 7th Madras joined the 6th Brigade under Major Langley. In 1790 Lord Cornwallis assumed command, and was joined by the Nizam's army in 1792. After the desultory warfare of the previous two years, the 7th Madras was sent to garrison duty in the Bangalore district, but appeared again in Col: Maxwell's force, sent to bring a recalcitrant Polygar to order at Thevagherry.

In February 1793, France declared war on England, and this led, as usual, to an attack by the Madras Government against Pondicherry. In this, the 7th was engaged, but it turned out a small affair, as operations commenced on August 10th, fire was opened on the 20th, and the place capitulated on the 22nd. In November 1794, the Battalion was engaged in the action against Manaar, in the Ceylon Expedition, and was present at the surrender of Colombo on February 15th 1796.

In this year, the reorganisation of the army took place, - one of many similar reorganisations - by which the 7th Regiment contained two Battalions; the 1/7th being formed of the 7th and Right wing of the 26th, and the 2/7th of the 20th and Left Wing of the 26th, each Battalion consisting of 8 Companies. As the 2/7th subsequently became the 19th M.N.I., it is not intended to include, in this history, any account of that unit.

The 7th had a detachment at the capture of Panjalamcoorchy in May 1801, and at the capture of the Perah Mally fort in July of that year, but the Headquarters were at Trichinopoly.

During 1804, it was found that the troops from the Bombay Presidency, employed in Malabar, were experiencing difficulty in the way of recruiting, and that the troops were inclined to be discontented, owing to the distance from their homes, and the lack of reliefs. As the same difficulties were not experienced by the use of troops from Madras, Lt. Col: Macleod was sent to relieve the discontented troops, with a respectable body of seven Battalions, including the 7th Madras, to that locality, in 1804.

In 1805 an order was issued by the C-in-C introducing a new pattern of turband, ostensibly to ensure a greater degree of uniformity. This seems to have been unnecessary, since, in 1797, the Military Board had gone thoroughly into the matter and had "given it every consideration which a subject of that delicate and important nature required". Early in 1806 another order was issued, which laid down that "a native soldier shall not mark his face to denote his caste, or wear earrings when dressed in his uniform.....and he shall be clean shaved on the chin. It is directed also that uniformity shall, as far as it is practicable, be preserved in regard to the quantity and shape of the hair on the upper lip". These orders had far-reaching effect, as dissatisfaction slowly but surely appeared, culminating in mutiny. One Battalion had many men who refused to wear the turband ordered, as being derogatory to caste, and of these men, two were tried and sentenced to 900 lashes each, and to be discharged as "turbulent and unworthy subjects". The remainder were given 500 lashes each, and then pardoned! The sedition, however, increased elsewhere, and the intention to mutiny in another unit, when reported to the C.O. by a sepoy, led to the latter being confined as insane. The lack of belief in possible disturbance, as held by the authorities is further shown by a case that occurred at Vellore. In this case, a woman, European, named Burke, endeavoured to apprise the local military authority that trouble was imminent: but when he learnt that she was a widow, he "bade her to go away, as he took her to be a bad woman". On July 10th the mutiny that she had tried to bring to his notice broke out, and was subsequently quelled. Those found guilty met their sentences in September. Among the sentences inflicted were, blowing from a gun, shooting, hanging, and transportation. During this mutiny at Vellore, the obnoxious orders were cancelled, and in September further instructions were issued preventing interference with the national observances of the native soldiery. Although the 7th did not appear in this, and similar incidents, reference has been made to it, on account of the far graver results that were later caused by the repetition of similar unwise orders. On this particular occasion, it led to the removal of both the Governor, and the C-in-C, in 1807.

The 7th Madras was stationed in various places until 1813, when it formed part of a force sent to Kuarnool to assist a political mission, which achieved its object.

It may be noted, that on November 2nd 1810, the first reward for officers who made themselves masters of the Hindostanee language was authorised.

In 1817, the Army of the Deccan was formed into 7 Divisions, and the 7th Madras became part of the 1st Inf: Bde: of the 1st Division. In that year the Battalion was in use against the Pindaries, and was left to garrison the fort of Hindia after its capture. In the subsequent actions, when the Pindaries were routed, we find that the standard of their chief, Cheetoo, "of red silk with a white crescent in the centre, measuring $13\frac{1}{2}$ feet by $11\frac{1}{2}$ feet, fell into the hands of the 1/7th." In 1818 the Battalion formed part of the force under Sir John Malcolm, in his operations against the Peshwa, Bajee Rao, after which it went into Cantonments in the rains, at Jaulna. Shortly, however, it was on the move again, to assist in operations in the Nagpore country, and it was present at the siege of Asseerghur on April 7th 1819, returning to Jaulna on May 5th.

During February 1819, the rank of Subadar Major was introduced into the Native Army, and also that of Colour Havildar.

The Battalion remained in peace stations until 1824, when, on May 23rd, it sailed from Madras, as part of the 4th Bde: of Madras troops, for Rangoon, where it landed on June 6th. It was actively employed in the First Burmese War, taking part in the actions against the town of Tavoy, in September 1824, and Mergui, in October 1824, and for it's services was among the units granted the reward of "Ava" on their colours. (See Appendix) In 1826 the Battalion returned to India. The following extract is from the despatch sent by the Governor in Council at Madras, on the war. ".......... the orders for foreign service were received with enthusiasm: whole regiments embarked without the deficiency of a man; and repeated instances occurred of extraordinary forced marches of parties absent from the Headquarters of a regiment about to embark, in order that they might not be left behind. Conduct so honourable to the Native Army, so gratifying to the Government, does not cease to be of use with the occasion which called it forth; it's influence will reach to future times, and it will be long regarded, both in India and Europe, as a memorable example for imitation to the sepoys, and for emulation to the successors of those European Officers who have made them what they are." Such words as these have proved to be curiously prophetic, to the later generations that had the handling of the sepoys in peace, and in War.

On arrival in India the Battalion was posted to Trichinopoly, where it remained until moved to Nagpore in 1829, thence proceeding to Bellary in 1835, and on to Kullanghee in 1838. In May 1841, four companies of the Battalion, under the command of Capt. Scotland, were employed in reducing the Fort at Badamee, which had been seized by a party of Arabs. In December of the same year, the Battalion returned to Secunderabad, remaining there until moved to Kamptee in January 1844. In 1846 the move was to Hoshungabad.

In this year, under instructions from the Honourable the Court of Directors, the facings of the Battalion were changed from French grey to sky blue; shoes, in place of sandals were introduced in 1848. It is not possible to state accurately whether these shoes were the "chappatu" shoes (the word is Tamil), or whether they were known by the Persian name "Paposh", but it appears to be unquestionable that these shoes were soon found to be of great use in the secreting of important messages, and transmitting them, without much risk of discovery. In 1849 new colours were presented to the Battalion by the O.C. Madras troops, Nerbudda and Jubbulpore Territories. In 1851 the Battalion moved to Jaulnah, and this year saw a change in the type of armament, from the flint lock to the percussion cap. In 1853, the Battalion moved to Vizianagram, and was ordered to Burma in November of the same year, arriving at Moulmein on May 1st 1854. In 1857 the move back to India took place, the station being Masulipatam, where heavy duties were called for in the way of detachments. The Battalion does not appear, from available records, to have taken any part in the Mutiny struggle, the only reference being to the receipt, in

1866, of Mutiny medals by 11 men who had in the meantime, been transferred from another unit to the 7th Madras.

In January 1859, the Battalion moved to Kamptee.

Many changes took place, up to 1861, in the ordered strength of battalions of the Native army, but these do not call for detailed category, being of frequent occurrence.

In 1863, the Battalion proceeded to Raipore and in the following year, new colours were presented by the wife of the officer Commanding the troops at that station. In 1865 the helmet was adopted for wear by European officers, on all parades, in place of the forage cap.

In 1867 the Battalion was ordered to Rangoon, and in 1869 the Headquarters moved to Singapore, leaving detachments behind, but the Battalion returned to Madras in 1871, and moved two years later to Vizagapatam. In March 1876, two companies were sent in aid of the Civil power to Jugdulpore, but were recalled, after marching 52 miles in 3 days!

The formation of a Regimental Band was authorized on January 1st, 1877, and in August of the same year, rearmament with Snider rifles took place. The work of formation of the Band took time, as it was not until 1879, when the Battalion was at Berhampore that the required instruments were received from England. Revolvers for Native officers were issued in 1881. During 1882 there were calls made for parties to proceed in aid of the Civil power, but there are no details of the work undertaken.

On April 1st 1883, the facings were once again changed, from sky blue to yellow. There were major alterations made during this year, in the uniform of the native ranks, which gave them khaki drill for every day dress, and the addition of red serge tunic, and khaki drill gaiters for full dress. The turband also became khaki.

Early in 1884 the Battalion moved to Kamptee. In the same year the first "puggree" of Regimental pattern, was introduced for British officers, and was ordered to be "of Tussore silk, 3 yards in length, and fourteen inches in width, bound in irregular folds on the helmet, the authorised brooch being affixed thereto." Further the numeral was changed from "VII" to "7" for the badge on the forage cap. (See Appendix)

On July 30th 1886 the Battalion left Kamptee by train, for Madras, taking up their lines there on August 4th and 5th. On 17th January 1887 the Battalion embarked for Rangoon, being split up into detachments on arrival, while the Headquarters and left wing landed at Port Blair on the 31st January. In November the Right Wing was closed, from detachment duties, at Rangoon.

A new Queen's Colour was received on July 3rd 1888, and Burma medals for service in 1885-1887, were presented to those entitled during November 1888. Early in 1889 the Battalion was moved to Toungoo.

On 26th April 1889, the battle honours "Carnatic" and "Mysore" were sanctioned for inscription on the colours (vide Appendix).

In 1890 the Battalion returned from Burma to India, and went to Mangalore. In November 1891, the adoption of a khaki "Kullah", by all native ranks, was sanctioned. In March 1892 a new badge was sanctioned, which contained the 3 battle honours, with the numeral "7" in the centre of the garter, the badge being worn on a yellow ground (that being the colour sanctioned for the facings). The badge was authorised to be worn on the front of the helmet, and to be in silver for British Officers and in brass for the Band and Drums. (See Appendix)

In this year, the Snider rifle was superseded by the Martini Henry Mk III Rifle.

In November 1892 the Battalion moved to Belgaum, and in 1895 a party was sent out to round up dacoits, which they successfully accomplished. 1896 saw the Battalion again in Kamptee and it took part in the assistance afforded the Civil power during the grain riots that occurred there. In 1898 the Battalion moved to Rangoon and Port Blair.

In May 1900 an important change in the system of organisation took place. The old "Wing" system was abolished, and the "Double Company" system was instituted in place. Under this system, the eight companies of a Battalion were linked into 4 pairs, each pair thus formed being termed a "Double Company". The 1st Double Company was commanded by the 2nd-in Command, the 2nd D.C. by the previous Wing Commander, and the 3rd and 4th D.Cs. by the two senior Wing Officers. The remaining British Officers were designated "Double Company Officers", and were allotted to the various Double Companies. The strength of the British Officers was laid down as:-

- 1 Commandant
- 4 Double Company Commanders
- 5 Double Company officers (of whom one was Adjutant, and one Quartermaster).

While the Double Company was thus made the administrative unit, the Company was the tactical unit, and the executive Command of Companies remained in the hands of Native Officers. It was further laid down that each Double Company should consist of two Companies of a similar class constitution, wherever possible. Where this was not possible, arrangements had to be made for linking Companies together in such a manner as would be most conducive to discipline, and efficiency, and in accordance with the religious and racial prejudices of the classes recruited.

On November 20th 1901, the Battalion left Rangoon, on return to India, and was posted to Vizianagram (Headqrs. and 2 Double Companies) and Cuttack (2 Double Companies).

In October 1902 the Headqrs, with Band and Drums, moved to Saugor C.P., to meet the needs of the new reconstruction that was already on the way.

In accordance with the instructions contained in G.G.O. No. 828 of 1902, the Battalion, as then constituted, was mustered out at Saugor, Vizianagram, and Cuttack, and the old 7th Madras Infantry, as it had been, ceased to exist, on November 14th 1902. The old Battalion had to make way for the New 7th Madras Infantry, which was ordered to be a Punjab-recruited Battalion, and which officially opened it's career in Saugor on November 15th 1902.

CHAPTER III

REPORTS. CRIMES AND PUNISHMENTS

Before leaving the old 7th Madras Infantry an opportunity is here taken of giving extracts from the old records, dealing with the matters forming the heading of this chapter, to provide some small sidelights on interior economy etc., which are not altogether devoid of humour as well as interest.

In the Report on the 1/7th Regiment Native Infantry dated at Madras, April 24th 1812, the following occur:-

" An irregular system of chewing and spitting beetle (sic), whilst under arms, prevails."

" The pieces were badly flinted."

" Two men of the same file should never be unloaded at the same time, one remaining to protect the other while reloading alternately." (The wording is different from, but the idea the same as, the present day teaching.)

In another report of the same year, we find that "the officers.... were ,... loud, decided, and pointed in the words of command." "The drummers and fifers beat, and play, tolerably well.

In the Field Return dated January 1820, there appears, under the heading of "Casualties" - " 9 men discharged, and 70 deserted." It is unfortunate that no other Field Return, about this time, is available for comparison. It seems quite possible that the two subheadings, which are contiguous, may have had their correct numbers interchanged!!

In the Confidential Report of 1824, occur two items of note. Referring to the Hospital the Inspecting Officer reports that "Vaccine Innoculation has not been introduced." In the General Remarks, it is observed that "The Mess is conducted with much propriety and respectability; and great cordiality seems to exist among the officers. The hour of dinner is at 7.0'clock, as recommended by His Excellency the Commander-in-Chief."

Turning now to Crimes and Punishments. Records both of the old 7th, and of the old army in India, present much that calls for more than a casual glance. To those who are conversant only with the present military Law, its methods and practice, some of the punishments here recorded will appear out of all proportion to the crime: and the changes which a century has brought about in this respect seem almost incredible. It may well be borne in mind, however, that these changes are not out of proportion, by any means, to those which have occurred in the Civil Criminal Code, in fact, the changes in the latter are even more startling. One need only recall how short the passage of years since the theft of a sheep, and offences of even less gravity, were rewarded with the death penalty. On the other hand, one may compare also the ease with which those guilty of fraud and embezzlement were able to defeat the ends of the law, with the heavy sentences now inflicted for similar offences.

The extracts following are taken from the return of 1819-20:-

(a) A sepoy, charged with sleeping on his post as sentry, and allowing thereby a musket to be removed from his care. 400 lashes. Inflicted.

(b) A sepoy, convicted of absence without leave from 10.6.1817, to his being handed over on 28.3.1819. 500 lashes. Inflicted.

(c) A sepoy, convicted of stealing a pair of long drawers from another sepoy. 500 lashes. Inflicted.

(d) A sepoy, convicted of being drunk and abusing the Cote-Havildar, and several sepoys of his company. 150 lashes. Inflicted.

(e) A sepoy convicted of
   (1) Refusing to obey an order.

   (2) Irregular conduct in quitting the ranks at a Public Guard-mounting without his turband. 350 lashes. Inflicted. Additional charge for disrespect to the Court during his trial, in saying that he would never wear his turband on his head again, nor would he do his duty: that the Adjutant might keep his turband, and that all the witnesses against him were liars

400 lashes. Only 150 of these were inflicted in view of the previous award.

(f) A sepoy, for entering the store tent at night, and stealing a piece of public iron therefrom, when he was posted as sentry. 500 lashes. Inflicted.

(g) A sepoy, for refusing to obey the orders of his Cote-Havildar, and seizing and pushing the said Havildar when in the execution of his duty. 50 lashes. Remitted. (But it may be noted that this was a sentence of a Line Court Martial, and that the Commanding Officer made some very caustic remarks about the sentence, in view of the magnitude of the crime).

Examples of clemency on the part of the Confirming Officer occur in the case of a Court Martial in 1824. In this case there is no record of the offence, but the Confirming Officer remitted 200 lashes in one instance, and in two instances the whole of the corporal punishment was remitted, and substituted punishment given, namely sepoy A "to dig a hole in the compound of the hospital to a depth of 5 feet, and of 2 feet square: and afterwards take extra duty for the number of days he may be so employed", and in the case of sepoy B, that he "shall dig a hole of 3 feet square and 2 deep, also taking extra duty for the time he may be so engaged": further, that until the ordered punishments were completed, the men concerned were to wear their regimental jackets turned inside out.

In 1824 a Native Regimental (or Line) Court Martial awarded a man six month's hard labour for stealing a bundle of firewood valued at four annas !

From the above extracts it will be seen that corporal punishment was used unsparingly in those days. Attempts to find conclusive evidence that the "cat" used, when so ordered, was the same as that of modern days, were not successful, but pursuit of the subject led to finding what is believed to be the heaviest sentence of corporal punishment known in the Army. In records kindly furnished for inspection by the India Office, and not in any way connected with the 7th Madras, it was found that a sergeant, convicted of inciting two drummers to desert, was sentenced to "2 months' solitary confinement and 1,000 lashes to be inflicted with the cat-o'-nine-tails". The writer has had some discussion with officers of the Royal Navy regarding some of the sentences, with a view to comparing them with that of "flogging round the fleet" as used in old days in the Senior Service. There was considerable divergence of opinion, and, no volunteers to put the matter to a practical test being forthcoming, no definite decision could be reached.

Both in life in the Services, and in Civil life, the question of abolition, or the retention, of corporal punishment has always been much discussed, and it is not likely that any consensus of opinion on such a subject will ever be found, but for that reason alone, it holds, and will always hold, interest. As regards the Indian Army, the infliction of corporal punishment, except for certain specified, and grave, offences, was abolished by the Commander-in-Chief in 1827. In 1835, on February 24th, the Governor General in Council (Lord William Bentinck) directed that "the practice of punishing soldiers of the Native Army by the cat-o'-nine-tails or rattan, be discontinued at all Presidencies, and that henceforth it shall be competent to any Regimental, Detachment, or Brigade Courts Martial, to sentence a soldier of the Native Army to dismissal from the service for any offence for which such soldier might now be punished by flogging."

In 1841, a small brochure was published in Calcutta by one Major N.H.Sleeman of the Bengal Native Infantry, and was entitled "On the spirit of Military Discipline in our Native Indian Army." Among the subjects dealt with in this brochure was the abolition of corporal punishment, and in view of the importance of the question both then, and now, no apology is made for giving extracts from the brochure, in this place. In the course of his enquiries, Major Sleeman was enabled to obtain the opinion of the senior Native Officer of his own Regiment, one Sheikh Mahoobalee Sirdar Bahadur, (1838), who had entered the Service at the age of 15, and had no less than 53 years service to his credit. His opinion is, therefore, worth quoting. He stated that the measure referred to had "made good men more careful, and bad men more orderly", in addition to reducing the number of Courts Martial, and thereby had lightened the duties of the officers. The reason he assigned for this effect was that " a bad man formerly went on recklessly from small offences to great ones, in the hope of impunity; he knew that no Regimental Cantonment, or Brigade Court Martial could sentence him to be dismissed the Service, and that they would not sentence him to be flogged except for great crimes, because it involved at the same time dismissal from the service. If they sentenced him to be flogged he still hoped that the punishment would be remitted. The General, or Officer confirming the sentence was generally unwilling for it to be carried into effect, because the man must, after being flogged, be turned out of the service, and the marks of the lash upon his back would prevent his getting service anywhere else. Now he knows that these Courts can sentence him to be dismissed from the service - that he is liable to lose his bread for ordinary transgressions; and be sentenced to work on the roads in irons for graver ones. He is, in consequence, much more under restraint than he used to be..... A man (who had been flogged) was disgraced not only before his regiment, but before the crowd that assembled to witness the punishment. Had he been suffered to remain in the regiment, he could never have hoped to rise, after being flogged, or sentenced to be flogged: his hopes were all destroyed, and his spirit broken: and the order directing him to be dismissed was good; but, as I have said, he lost all hope of getting into any other service, and dared not show his face among his family at home". Apart from these, there were many other important factors which carried weight in the matter. For instance, the funeral obsequies offered up to the shades of deceased parents in September of each year, were not considered acceptable from the hands of a soldier who had been flogged; and, provided he was the head of a family, he thereby lost his civil rights, - for, by presiding at such ceremonies alone, was he able to secure and maintain his recognition. The old soldier, however, was of opinion that, for recruits at drill, the rattan was not only advisable, but necessary. He says that no one objected and that "young men were formerly, with the judicious use of the rattan, made fit to join the Regiment at furthest in 6 months: but since the abolition of the rattan, it takes 12 months to make them fit to be seen in the ranks".

The ideas put forward by the old soldier seem worthy of consideration - but, as has been observed, the question is one that is not likely ever to be settled by an overwhelming majority of opinion, one way or the other.

Solitary confinement as a possible part of a Court Martial award, was first introduced into the native army in 1856.

CHAPTER IV

THE NEW 7TH MADRAS INFANTRY (67TH PUNJABIS)

The new Battalion came into being, under the same order as that which authorised the mustering out of the old. The 7th, 9th and 14th Madras Infantry were replaced by the new units bearing the same designation; but with 'class Companies' composition under a new constitution. This consisted of:-

```
4 Cos. P.M.
2  "   Sikhs (other than Jats or Mozbis).
2  "   Punjabi Hindus.
```

In order to provide a nucleus, each of the new units was authorised to draw 200 transfers, from Punjab, Bengal, Burma or Bombay Infantry regiments, which recruited the named classes. Orders were laid down regarding the various tribes from which the classes were to be made up, but subsequent changes so occurred as to make the enumeration of the original tribes of no present value. It is worthy of note, that the reconstituting Order states that "to facilitate recruitment, the Government of India sanction the bestowal of four Jemadars' Commissions, in each regiment, on native gentlemen of good family of the classes named, provided they can bring for enlistment 50 approved recruits." The four in the 7th M.I. were taken pro rata to strength of classes authorised. From the old unit, only two P.Ms. came to the new, one of whom was the Armourer, who was an exceptionally good one. The three new units were formed into a linked-battalion group, with the Regimental centre at Bangalore. The uniform of all three was fixed as red, with green facings, and to be assimilated in every respect except badges and buttons.

The 7th M.I. was reconstituted at Saugor, on 15th November, 1902, and arrangements were immediately made for British Officers, and men received, or selected, on transfer, to proceed to the authorised districts for recruiting purposes. The recruiting was decentralised, and all details were left in the hands of Major A. W. Newbold, 2nd in Command, and Lt. Col. Burton, I.M.S., the Medical Officer. These officers carried out their duty with rapidity and thoroughness, and the battalion was practically recruited in two months' time. The C.O.

Lt. Col. G. W. Maxwell, found no difficulty in getting recruits to fill vacancies, and there was a good waiting list. In later years, the question of recruiting was not always so satisfactory, but when recruits failed to come to Regimental Headquarters in sufficient numbers, the Recruiting Staff Officers, in the various districts concerned, were invariably able to assist in providing the requirements. To any one who has not taken a part in the raising of a new regiment, the multiplicity of detail that has to be examined, the sometimes tedious delays after a decision has been reached, and the difficulties of combining with two other units, (stationed elsewhere), in deciding the various matters of uniform and equipment (except badges and buttons), would form a useful portion of education. It was not a matter entirely in the hands of the B.Os., as the Native Officers, as they were then called, had also to be consulted; in order that nothing should be decided which might prejudice Mahomedan or Hindu. It was not easy - at times it was far from easy - but the wholehearted loyalty with which everyone concerned worked for the common end, smoothed out difficulties in a surprising way. In addition to the requirements of the men, questions of badge, devices, colours, and many other similar, had to be solved. As regards the colours of the regimental tie etc., we were indebted to the selection of the C.O's wife, and it was accepted by the other two battalions interested. Records regarding the formation of the Band are, unfortunately not in existence, but certain humorous incidents therewith connected come to mind - the promise of a watch to the Bandmaster (a retired British N.C.O.) if the Band could function at Mess by a certain date. He got the watch, but recollection of the occasion leads to think it might have been better if the date had been postponed!! After being allowed to train for nearly two years, the Battalion was ordered in the reliefs, to proceed, in October 1904, by route march to Fort Lockhart.

The march was about 1100 miles, and was started on Oct. 10, 1904, ending on Feb. 21st, 1905. Normally, there is not much worthy of record in a march on relief, but in this case it was different. For one thing, the march itself was a new experience to 75% of the Battalion. The opening phases were delightful - due to the presence of plague on the normal marching road, the unit was ordered to go as far as Jhansi, by the old Lalitpur road. This had not been used by troops since the Mutiny, and consequently the local folk were not well up in the routine of things required. This lead to some humorous incidents. It was the duty of the Quarter Master of the battalion, a British officer, to go ahead of the unit to the next camping ground, with the camp site party, and see that the required supplies were ready, and then to lay out the camp with flags, and lines on the ground. Mistakes at first did occur, but not grave ones, and in a very short time this duty could be completed in a very brief space of time, as the party were kept the same, and got to know how to work in quickly with the measurements. On one occasion, the Quarter Master reached a very spacious grass camping ground, at one end of which was a fine grove of mango trees. It was obviously the place for the Officers' tents and Mess, but inspection showed that the ground was gravel, in the grove, and that it had been carefully levelled and rolled. Enquiries from the Tehsildar or village headman, elicited the reply that it was presumed that the British Officers would like to play polo there! On another occasion, the Tehsildar, according to old custom, held out a rupee in his hand, for the Quarter Master to "touch and remit" (Nazrana). The custom only means "services offered and accepted", but the young officer was not aware of the custom, and, after carefully examining the rupee, asked what was wrong with it, and why it was offered to him? Explanations followed, much to his embarrassment!! There was a good deal of shooting available, and this was much enjoyed by Officers, and Indian Officers, and this portion of the march was particularly pleasant. In further stages, on roads that were in constant use for troops marching in relief, there was a lack of such diversion, except to a very limited extent. On arrival at Jhansi, the Battalion was kept there to take part in manoeuvres for 3 weeks, and a good experience, although the manoeuvres were really for a Cavalry force. The weather on the whole was clement, but beyond Lahore, heavy rains had made the camping grounds morasses, and the tents had to be pitched on the sides of the road, three marches in succession. The itinerary of the march had been carefully made out, and printed, and in this very arduous task, (Route Books are not quite as accurate as might be expected) the greatest help was given by an Indian Officer, Jem: Sukha Singh, a Khatri Sikh of very high educational attainments, who had transferred on promotion, from the 13th Watsons' Horse. His knowledge of English was exceptional, and his writing both rapid and very clear. In preparing this itinerary, the C.O.

had arranged to make the extra day's halt, which came at intervals, at military stations, where it would be possible for the exchange of civilities with other units, or at a place in the heart of our own recruiting districts, where men could avail themselves of 36 hours leave to see their homes and friends. Throughout the march, under the supervision of the British Officers, wherever it was possible to find a suitable bit of ground, hockey was played in the afternoon, and at every Military station, matches were arranged with some Indian unit there stationed. It was all to the good of the young regiment, and they acquited themselves well in these games, nearly always coming out victors. On occasions, it was found possible to turn out a complete team of British Officers - no mean feat, when the total number, including the M.O. was only 14 !! This marching, although at times tedious, was unsuspectedly having a very good result in making the men fit, and the Daily State of Sick on Feb: 21st 1905, was, according to memory only, one man. Our Xmas Day 1904, was spent on the battle field of Panipat, where the fate of India was three times decided. On arrival at Fort Lockhart, a new phase in the education of the Battalion was introduced, that of Mountain Warfare training, and in one of the first efforts in this practice, when the Battalion took its place, in the manoeuvres with the Kohat Brigade, in the mountainous area, the results of the march, in the fitness of the men, was evident. They were able to hold their own with the seasoned troops of the Frontier Force, and the latter were not so slow to acknowledge that they were genuinely surprised, and appreciated, this capability. For the 7th M.I. were the first Non-Frontier unit to be stationed among the Frontier Force. A few words may be said here, regarding the difficulties experienced during the march, in the matter of transport. Instead of being given Government A.T.Carts, a new form was brought in for trial, and the new unit was selected for the 'try out'. The system consisted of being supplied, through the Civil authorities, with the required amount of transport of a country nature, to carry the authorised maundage. But this had to be taken over on reaching the near boundary of any particular civil district, and paid off on reaching the further boundary, where the fresh transport was supplied from the next district, and so on. The idea of impressing his transport did not appeal to the local inhabitant, neither did the form of the transport supplied, at one place, bear necessarily a resemblance to that being discharged! There would be 4-bullock wagons, 2-bullock carts, and single bullock carts, and some mules, or camels, or anything. Although the transport provision was the duty of the Civil authorities, it often happened that even when the required amount had been collected overnight, it would be found considerably diminished in the morning. Sometimes the owners took away their carts, bullocks and all, and sometimes only the bullocks. As the march was worked by a set itinerary, which had to be followed in order to keep straight with the supplies, these defalcations made things very hard. But, in spite of it all, there was only one occasion where a hold-up of a complete day occurred, and that was relieved by the unholy joy of the C.O. and Quartermaster in expending 250 Rupees of Government money, in ensuring the matter being rectified by the end of 24 hours. It was! From other sources, it is believed that, later, the method worked comparatively smoothly, but it was not so on its first trial. It meant heavy work in calculation and distribution to sub-units, and became at times almost a nightmare to those who had to get the tangle straight in time. Throughout the year spent at Fort Lockhart, which was the hill station for Kohat, one Double Company was detached at Thall, the railhead of the line from Kohat, at the beginning of the Kurram Valley, and another small detachment at Hangu, the station for Fort Lockhart. In Fort Lockhart, the Battalion was on a historic ridge, close to the scene of the Saragarhi disaster, and in touch with various posts held by the Samana Rifles. It was a good training ground for troops up from the plains, although the drill ground was very small. But interesting people were frequently passing through, and there was more than enough to keep one fully occupied. In March 1906 the Battalion moved to Kohat, a pleasant station, and after living for some time in the big Frontier Force Mess, set up their own. Here the Battalion stayed for nearly 3 years, improving its knowledge of Mountain Warfare, and taking an active part in the many trials and experiments that were being tested and introduced in that essential form of Warfare for the defence of India. The next station was Multan in the Punjab, where the Battalion arrived on 28 January 1909. This was another complete change, as Multan is one of the hottest places in the Punjab. But it had its compensations, particularly for the men. Both Fort Lockhart and Kohat were too far from the recruiting areas of more than half the unit, to permit of them obtaining short leave to their homes. From Kohat, certain of the P.M. tribes were favourably placed in this respect, but not so others, nor the Sikhs, nor the Punjabi Hindus. So the latter classes were able to avail themselves from Multan as they could not do further North. In addition to its deserved reputation for heat, dust storms, and lack of water, Multan has also got a name for being "a good spot if you have got the right people". In the time the Battalion was there this essential was provided. The British batteries, and line regiment, the Indian Cavalry, and the other Indian Regiment, were all "the right people", and there was no suspicion of the internal friction that can mar even a good station, and make a poor one unbearable. Training and manoeuvre grounds were not as good as they might have been, but lessons hitherto unlearnt, were provided in the work necessary to ensure profitable results in working over heavy sand dunes, particularly at night! There was not an undue amount of sickness, and the possibilities for sport and games of all kinds were fully utilised. On the whole, Multan was not unkind, and the Battalion might well have been worse placed. The next move took place in November 1911, to Quetta, Baluchistan, where the unit arrived on the 18th of the month. Here, once more, was a distinct change. From the dead plain level, at Sibi, the railway climbs over 5,000 ft. to the Quetta plateau, and there is practically no hot weather at that altitude, though August can be uncomfortable. But from about the beginning of January, until the middle of March, the plateau is subject to severe cold, and swept by biting wind that comes down through the passes on the North, and will go through any heavy clothing. This was the first time that the unit came into what may be called a "full Division" station, with opportunities to meet and study new conditions, and take their part in a higher type of training, as regards numbers and areas employed, than had hitherto been possible. It was years later that Quetta became a Command Headquarters, with a large Air Force depot: but it was quite big enough, even then. The facilities there afforded for training in conjunction with other areas, for specialist training, and improvement, were manifold, and the fruits of this were shown later when the Battalion took its part in the Great War. The rugged Mountainous Country surrounding the Quetta Plateau, gave further employment in Mountain Warfare, and the proximity of the Staff College gave opportunities to Officers who were anxious to increase their knowledge by the many lectures offered and given to the garrison from that source. Games were available with different units, and were very constantly enjoyed. The Battalion remained in Quetta till August 9th 1914, when it moved to Loralai, one of the "outpost" stations in the Zhob Area. Both from Quetta and from Loralai, detachments were provided in some numbers, and it may be mentioned that, with the exception of that provided from Quetta, to Robat, on the Nushki Railway (which was a half Battalion Detachment) these were all under Indian Officers or Non Commissioned Officers. It will be conceded, that such work was of the greatest value, in imbuing these Detachment commanders with the sense of responsability that makes a commander, and that therefore, Quetta and Loralai proved excellent stations for the furthering of this training. When orders came for active service, the Battalion was at Loralai.

LOWER MESOPOTAMIA
BETWEEN BAGHDAD AND THE PERSIAN GULF

CHAPTER V

THE GREAT WAR - MESOPOTAMIA

Before chronicling the actual operations of the Regiment in Mesopotamia, for it was in that region that most of their active service was done, it is advisable to look briefly at the causes which led to the Campaign in that country being undertaken. Wars and campaigns in it were no new thing, and although Baghdad and Basra are more well known as the scenes of the doings of the mythical "Arabian Nights" and "Sinbad the Sailor", the name we use for the district shows the influence of the Greeks. Mesopotamia means " between the rivers" i.e. between the Tigris and Euphrates, and it was in the Tigris Valley that Xenophon led the lost army of the Greeks in the Retreat of the Ten Thousand until they hailed the sight of the friendly sea in the distance. After Suleiman the Magnificent had conquered Baghdad in the Seventeenth century, the land between that city and the Persian Gulf became a part of the Ottoman Empire, and remained so until our own times. But even in the days of Queen Elizabeth, Englishmen had visited the Persian Gulf by sea. The interest of the Gulf, to Britain, was considerable on account of its proximity to India, and during the nineteenth century English influence was much extended: surveys, buoying of the Gulf by the Royal Navy, and the placing of political residents at various points all strengthened this interest far beyond that originally taken by the East India Company in the possession of a station at Bunder Abbas near the mouth of the Gulf, in the seventeenth century. Shortly before the outbreak of the world war, these interests were further increased by the opening and working of valuable oil fields in this region, by the Anglo-Persian Oil Company. It was announced in 1913 that the Admiralty had secured a controlling interest in these wells, when oil was beginning to be used extensively as fuel for ships. Prior to this, the German firm of Wonckhaus & Company, had secured a foothold in the Gulf in 1901, and had, by various means extended their dealings, and in 1906, the firm appeared in the open as representatives of the Hamburg-Amerika Line, when the firm began to run a line of steamers to the chief Gulf ports. But the ideas of Germany as regards this region did not rest in the activities of the firm of Wonckhaus & Co. - her scheme was the construction and control of the Baghdad Railway, to link up the Persian Gulf with the Mediterranean Sea, and, with the assent of the Turkish Government, a company had been formed, backed by German money, to carry out the work.

And so it happened, that when the German Government succeeded in enlisting Turkey on their side in 1914, the Turkish Government was placed in the difficult position of risking her various possessions, from Constantinople to the Gulf. It can be readily understood, then, why an Expeditionary Force to Mesopotamia was advisable; and, though various historians yet fail to agree, it seems that the reasons given above are more likely to be correct, than the contention that the Campaign was only taken up to form a success as against the failure in the Dardanelles, and bolster up the British prestige in the Orient. The force sent originally, under Sir Arthur Barrett, consisted of one division, with auxiliary troops. Basra was formally entered, after some fighting, on 23rd November, 1914, and on 8th December our troops were in possession of Mezera and Kurna, the former on the left bank of the Tigris, opposite Kurna, which was at the point where the two rivers joined, and which was also said by some to be the original site of the Garden of Eden. This theory appears to have been, however, amply disproved. The next move was the despatch of a force to Ahwaz, a town on the left bank of the Karun river, which was of importance owing to its proximity to the pipelines, that led the oil from the wells to the refinery at Abadan, situated at the point where the Karun enters the Shat-el-arab. The authorities in India then sent further reinforcements to Ahwaz and Kurna.

After the decisive victory of the British forces at Shaiba, on 14th April, the Turks really began their retreat, and it was only near Kurna and Ahwaz, that they still remained troublesome though it was certain that operations would also be necessary on the Euphrates later. It was to the force collected at Ahwaz, subsequently forming the XII Division, that the 67th Punjabis were first allotted on their long tour of active service in Mesopotamia and elsewhere.

In order that the reader may have some idea of the trying conditions under which the troops in Mesopotamia carried out their duties, and their fighting, a brief description of the country may be useful. In the ancient times, the country between Basra, and Baghdad, was one of the most fertile regions on the face of the globe. But after the Mongols, Arab nomads, and Turks had swept across it, the tract between the two great rivers had deteriorated into wastes of sand, and swamp. It was not difficult to see why neither the Turks from the north, where they had a large garrison at Mosul, nor any invaders from the Gulf, had been able to occupy this wilderness. The Rivers flooded at certain times of the year, and the intervening country thus became largely swamp land. Although the thermometer did

not register any higher degree of temperature than in many
places in the Punjab, the swamps gave a high humidity to
the heated air. In addition, the marsh Arabs, who inhabited these swamp areas, and were indifferent to hygiene
and sanitation, filled the surrounding swamps with rotting
refuse and filth of every description. The natural result
was that these places became fertile breeding places for
unbelievable swarms of mosquitoes, biting flies and vermin,
and the dry areas harboured millions of the equally dangerous sand fly. It is no exaggeration to say that an equally
definite war had to be waged against these enemies, as against the human Turk and Arab foes. The local Arabs, rendered immune by centuries of living among these pests, took
no heed, and but little harm, from them; but the British,
Indian, and even Turkish, troops suffered from insect-borne
diseases in many forms. Of all, the flies were perhaps
the worst, eating was rendered difficult by them, and their
attentions produced dysentery, and made life unbearably hard.
The humidity of the air, the heat of the sun, and the insects
of all sorts wrought havoc with sickness among the troops,
both British and Indian. As one historian remarks, "The
campaign in East Africa was not exactly a picnic, but that
in Mesopotamia was a nightmare". The amount of water to
be met, and crossed, or overcome, called for the utmost
ingenuity on the part of the Royal Navy, Royal Indian Marines,
and Royal Naval Reserve, in turning the campaign in its
early days, and indeed almost throughout, into a kind of amphibious warfare. The river craft brought gradually into
use, for the transport of troops, food, sick etc., were extremely varied. Paddle boats from the Irrawaddy, "cast"
sloops from the Navy, punts, barges, motor boats, tugs, the
river craft of the firm of Lynch, Bros., from Basra, Thames
penny steamers, and later specially built first class river
boats, all were brought into constant use. Nor must be
forgotten the only one of its type, an ex-aeroplane, devoid
of wings, which became a launch with an aerial propeller,
and travelled with a noise like a badly backfiring motorcycle!
In addition, men had to be taught how to manipulate the local
Arab craft, "bellums", which varied in size and beam, but
were eminently useful in the marshes. The further the
British forces advanced, the longer grew the line of river
communications; and the greater the need of more, and yet
more craft, until the time finally came when the capture of
Baghdad, and the settling down of Lower Mesopotamia, made it
possible to lay a railway, first from Basra to Kut. In a
letter sent by an officer from the force to England, he stated
that in the course of two years in Mesopotamia he had experienced all the ten plagues of Egypt, "except the death of the
first-born".

One of the most difficult types of operations was that connected with hunting down and harassing the local unfriendly Arabs. It was not long before they learnt all our cavalry methods, and resorted to the same tactics as the Arabs had used for centuries against the Mongol, Persian, Assyrian and other forces. They went off in to the desert, where they knew of hidden water, and on occasions the pursuers were finally led up against - thirst, as they could not locate the water known to Arabs. Many are the authenticated stories of such happenings during the campaign, and it was aggravated by the dry sandy stretches where the sun above and the sand below appeared to dry up all the fluid in the body, rendering perspiration impossible, and at times producing a state of coma. The use of aeroplanes, and pack wireless, further assisted by armed motors, where the sand was firm enough for their use, did much towards altering the conditions, and the Arabs discovered that they could not pursue their old tactics with anything like the same success. Raids on outlying Arabs, were rendered possible, and they were given no respite, and these measures lead to the rapid "conciliation" of the occupied territory.

On the evening 6/7th March, 1915, telegraphic orders were received for the Battalion to be prepared to move overseas, as a portion of Force "D", on the understanding that the move received the necessary support from the Political Officer. This was given, and mobilisation began. At this time the battalion was much split up into detachments, which made the concentration more difficult, but the Battalion was able to move from Loralai on the 16th March, en route to Kiamari, which was reached on 21st March, on which day it embarked on H.T. "Aronda" for Busra, arriving there on 25th March, slightly under strength, owing to the inability to gather in all detachments without causing undue delay in starting. It was unfortunate that one of the ship's crew developed smallpox during the voyage between India and Mesopotamia, as this led to the Battalion having to go into quarantine at Magil for three weeks, changing camp to Makina Masus about half time. On April 8th orders were received for the Battalion to join the 12th Brigade XII Division at Ahwaz, on the Karun River, and this point was reached by river on 11th April. The force at Ahwaz was located there, on the right flank of the force in, Mesopotamia, to prevent any move round by that flank, on the part of the Turks, who had a small force in the vicinity.

The threat never materialised, as the defeat of the Turks at Shaiba, on 12th to 14th April, 1915, finally stopped any possibility. The force in the vicinity however were able to make the camp at Ahwaz uncomfortable, which they did by intermittent shelling, which appeared to be aimed chiefly at the shipping lying in the River Karun, behind the camp. This Turkish force was discovered, by reconnaissance on the 22nd of April, to have left its previous camp, and it was later decided that the Ahwaz force should push westward, across the desert, and deal with hostile Arab tribes, and dispel hostile gatherings en route. The march was started on 3rd May, the Brigade proceeding to Imamzada, where the 12th Division Headquarters, and remainder of troops were located. The lack of transport was felt, but it had been found essential for the Division to have a Bridging train, which followed the 12th Brigade from Ahwaz. On the way the tractor broke down, and the Battalion was ordered to proceed with all available wheeled transport to rescue the Bridging train, and if necessary jettison the tractor. Several hours of search in great heat by B.Os. mounted, finally located the tractor quite near its original starting point Ahwaz. At 4.15 p.m., i.e. 12 hours after the "fall-in", the march was resumed with Bridging train transferred to ordinary wheeled transport, but at 5 p.m. the tractor again broke down, and had to be abandoned. The Batallion eventually succeeded in getting the Bridging train to camp at 11-30 p.m. This was a good day's work: 19 hours in full equipment, doing both protective and fatigue duties, covering 25 miles bad going in great heat, and not a man falling out. The Battalion always referred to the day as "The Puffing Billy Stunt." On the 8th, the Brigade moved to Illah, on the bank of the old Kharkeh River, and the Battalion was able to provide several expert swimmers to assist in getting horses, and mules, over the river, as the Bridging train could not provide a bridge for animals. On the 13th the Battalion took part in the operations against a local town and marsh city, called Khafajiyeh, which was to be destroyed in view of its hostile population. The march was slow, owing to the numerous creeks that had to be bridged before the column could cross. The marsh Arabs always felt they were safe in the marshes, and the tribe implicated in this case, the Beni Turuf, had been with the Turks against us, and had an unsavoury reputation for cruelty to the wounded that fell into their hands. The burning of their head village was a very unpleasant surprise for them, and was no easy task for the troops concerned. Khafajiyeh was destroyed on May 16th and the Brigade remained in that vicinity for 10 days, moving further west to Bisaitin on the 28th May. Here the Battalion remained until June 9th. On that date, the 12th Division split, Headquarters and remainder returning to Ahwaz, and the 12th Brigade, consisting of 7th Hariana Lancers 82nd Battery, R.F.A., 1/st Royal West Kent Regiment, 67th Punjabis and 90th Punjabis, with auxiliary details, proceeding over the desert to Amara on the Tigris. Of this march, little has been heard, save from those who took part in it: but it was recognised on its merits by the Mesopotamian "Eyewitness" and deserves detail in some measure. Although there was no fighting, it was not any easy journey. The time of year was intensely hot, and day marching was not feasible. Marches took place therefore at about 4.30 - 8 a.m. and about 6 - 9 p.m. It was over open desert, and sand, and the available water supply was marsh water. On one occasion the 82nd Battery were unable to water horses till 10 p.m. owing to the high temperature of the water, which the horses would not drink, and then followed the column with an infantry escort. The cavalry moved half a march ahead, and sent back guides for the column, to each halting place. On occasions the transport had to be lightened by throwing off loads of bhoosa before they could make headway at all. In addition carriage had to be found for men who were overcome by heat on the march. On June 13th the column arrived on the edge of a broad expanse of swamp that had to be crossed, where a company of the 48th Pioneers had been sent with rafting materials and a collection of local marsh Arabs' craft (Mahsufs) to assist the crossing. The guns and A.T. carts were transported on rafts, and in boats, into which were also placed the arms, accoutrements and equipment of the men; while horses, mules, and men had to wade. Men of small stature, like some of the Dogras in the Battalion were compelled to hang on to these boats as they were poled across, the water being too deep for them to wade. The objective of the crossing, was to reach the bank of the large Jalalieh canal, flowing from the Tigris at Amara, into the desert. Along this bank, the march of 12 miles into Amara was good going. Every effort was made to ensure safe crossing of the swamp, but the Battalion unfortunately lost 2 men drowned. As the route to Amara was not known, Capt. Colan of the 67th was sent to reconnoitre, and was ambushed by Arabs on his way back, having his horse shot under him, and he himself escaping with difficulty. The force, at the end of this most strenuous march, arrived at Amara on June 15th. This town, an important one 60 miles up stream from the junction of the two great rivers, had been captured by a force sent up from the Junction point Kurna, after a series of wonderful amphibious attacks, on June 3rd. A close study of those operations will well repay the student, in the acquired knowledge of the way the difficulties were overcome by the "amphibious" method. After the conclusion of the march to Amara, the 67th were ordered to Basra, and proceeded by river steamer, arriving on June 19th. Kurna, referred to above, is the last steamer halt before Basra, and is locally reputed to be the site of the Garden of Eden. It was a most unsanitary spot, swarming with mosquitoes, and uncomfortable in every way. It is, therefore, easy to understand the humorous opinion of Mr Thomas A that if it was the Garden of Eden "it wouldn't have needed any flaming sword to keep me out of it." At Basra, the Battalion was allotted duties in connection with the safety of the city, and there remained, in camp, until July 8th, refitting and equipping generally. The climate was hot, and damp, and not at all pleasant - due to the marshes round, the inundated palm groves, and consequent humidity; it did not compare at all favourably with the more congenial air at Amara. The Turkish force, which had, on April 14th, been defeated at Shaiba, had retreated up the Euphrates, to Nasiriyeh, where they were joined by reinforcements, including artillery drawn from Adrianople. During the flood season, the Euphrates line formed the only possible line of an advance on Basra, and the town of Nasiriyeh was an important one, not only in itself, but as the capital of the warlike tribe of Muntifik Arabs. Its junction with the Shat El Hai canal, running between the Euphrates, and the Tigris, opposite Kut to the North, added much to its military importance. The capture of the town would mean the closing of the only route of attack on Basra, during the flood season, and would render the position secure for the time. The Turks had made strong preparations against an attack, being entrenched on both sides of the river, and further down had detachments along the old channel of the Euphrates which runs through a large sheet of water known as the Hamar Lake, to the junction with the Tigris at Kurna. From December, 1914 there had been skirmishing between our steamers and motorboats, along this water, and gradually the enemy were forced back on Nasiriyeh, and the Arab snipers cleared out of the lake. The final stretch to the Euphrates proper (new channel junction with old channel) was cleared by the beginning of July, and arrangements were made, then, for organised operations against the town.

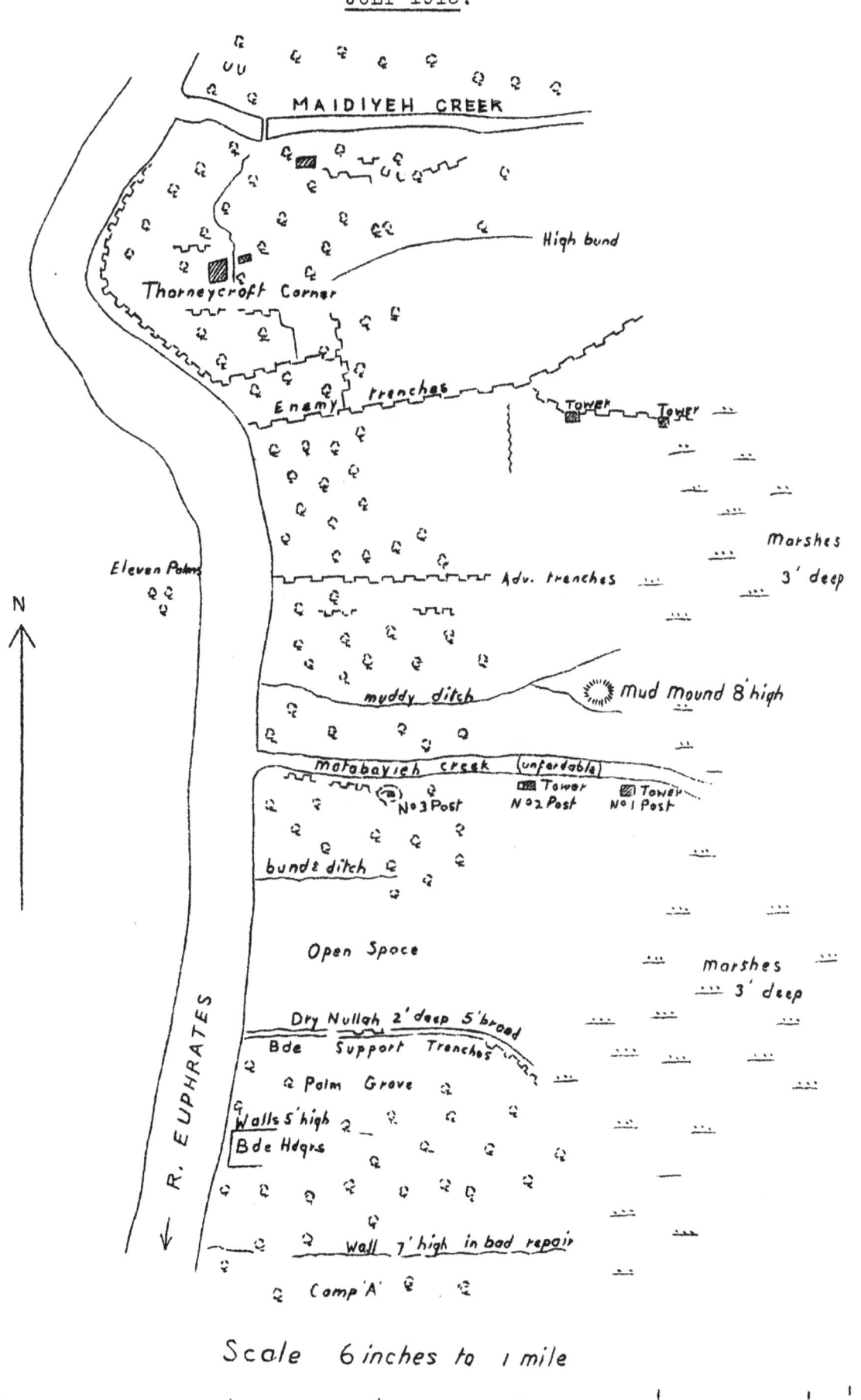

CHAPTER VI

THE GREAT WAR - MESOPOTAMIA. OPERATIONS AT NASIRIYEH

On 8th July orders were received for the Battalion to embark, for these operations, as a unit of the XII Division, under General Gorringe, who had the 12th and 30th Brigades, with auxiliary troops. The Turks had placed a dam at the entrance to the Hamar Lake, across which the force had to move, and it was only possible to get the river boats through the break made in the dam, (where the water flowed like a mill race) by disembarking troops, and turning them on to man drag ropes, and so assist the steamers through. The force eventually concentrated at a point seven miles below Nasiriyeh, and it was arranged that when the attack was ready to be launched, the 12th Brigade would attack on the left, and the 30th Brigade on the right bank. The Battalion reached the concentration point on 11th July. The Turks were in strength against the Division, and for some days heavy firing took place, and local attacks were made, but without any appreciable result. The Battalion were on out-post duty in their turn, and during their relief by the 90th Punjabis on 14th, heavy fire was opened by the enemy, with the result that Captain Atkins was slightly wounded, one I.O. and three men killed, and 38 wounded. Throughout this period of waiting, considerable annoyance was caused nightly by marsh Arabs, who came in boats to the edge of the marsh (which extended Northwards, from the right of our position) firing in enfilade and even from the rear, and then making off into the marsh at dawn. The infantry units of the Brigade (1st Royal West Kents, 67th and 90th Punjabis) took, in turn, two days in the front trenches, and four out. Fatigues and working parties were unceasing, for those not occupying the front line. There was the usual daily firing but the casualties were negligible. On the 23rd July, orders were issued for the attack on Nasiriyeh, the following day. At 5 a.m. on the 24th, the bombardment of the enemy's trenches on the left bank started, and ceased at 5.30 a.m., when the Royal West Kents advanced from our front line trenches against the enemy position, which rested on the river, on their right, and was partly protected by barbed wire. The advance was made in half Battalion waves, the Royal West Kents being followed by the 90th Punjabis, and the 67th coming up behind the latter, in

Reserve. By 6.30 a.m. Nos. 1 and 4 D.Cs., under Captain H.N.Colan, were in the advanced trenches, the remainder of the Battalion being in their original position in rear. While the first stages of the attack were in progress, 2/Lt. Arbuthnott noticed some of the M.G.mules of another unit had broken loose, and with a party, went out and succeeded in getting them back, in spite of heavy enemy firing. At 7 a.m. the half Battalion under captain Colan, was sent up to support the Royal West Kents, who were held up after capturing the first two lines of the enemy's trenches. In the meantime the 90th Punjabis had moved forward on the right of the Royal West Kents. The remainder of the Battalion with Headquarters under Major Cox, now moved up to our original front line trenches. At 7.30 a.m. this portion of the Battalion was able to assist the attack of the 30th Brigade on the right bank, by enfilade fire across the river. On the left of the enemy line, were two towers, and the half Battalion under Major Cox, went up to the attack with these towers as their objective, but the order was cancelled, as it was seen that the 90th Punjabis had taken these towers into their own attack. Major Cox then was ordered to take his half Battalion up to fill the gap between the right of the Royal West Kents and the left of the 90th. The situation was, then, the left attack carried on by the Royal West Kents supported by the half Battalion 67th under Captain Colan; Headquarters and remaining half Battalion 67th in the centre, and the 90th Punjabis on the right. Then No. 4 D.C. from Captain Colan's half Battalion, rejoined Headquarters under Major Cox in the centre. The remaining D.C. (No. 1) still on the left in support of the Royal West Kents made good the opportunity of firing heavily on the Turks evacuating their trenches on the right bank of the river, under the pressure of the attack of the 30th Brigade. It was seen by Major Cox that the attack was held up by the determined resistance to his front, and he therefore ordered his three D.Cs. to attack directly over the 'high bund' (see sketch map). In the heavy fire that was the enemy's reply to this action, Major Cox was wounded in the head, and the three D.Cs. were led on by the next in command on the spot, Captain Gribbon, who, after a series of short rushes, sent his men in with the bayonet. In the trenches, this officer actually seized the rifle of a fighting Turk in his left hand, belabouring the man with his sword in the right hand, but failed, in spite of his great personal strength, to wrest the rifle away from the owner, who was bayonetted by our men during the struggle.

The Turks retreated, on this attack, by a crazy bridge, and our attack was held up by the Maidiyeh Creek, but it was not difficult to shoot down every Turk who tried to cross the bridge. This was the first objective successfully attained. On our left the Royal West Kents and No. 1 D.C. of the 67th, were still engaged with stubborn parties, in Thorneycroft Corner, but the Turks there, realising that their retreat over the Maidiyeh Canal was now impossible, surrendered. Captain Colan then brought his D.C. to rejoin the Battalion, and took over command, being next senior to Major Cox. During this attack, the regimental Bhisties followed up the reputation of the immortal "Gunga Din", by carrying drinking water up and down to the fighting troops. It was clear that the attack was not expected, as the Turkish Gunners Headquarters were passed in the advance, with the bedclothes still on the beds, and the early tea lying untouched. The Brigade Commander expressed his personal thanks, at this period, to the Battalion for their share in the attack. The 67th now became the leading battalion of the Brigade, and the advance was continued, at first without opposition, until it was seen that another creek, directly across the line of advance, was the next obstacle to be overcome. This was the Sadanawiyeh creek, and on the north of it was visible the enemy's next line of defence. So far four enemy field guns had been captured; two more were visible in the position now disclosed, and any effort to remove them was stopped by marksmen keeping up a well directed fire on them. Reconnaissance of the position by patrols was rendered ineffective by the Turkish fire, as the ground was quite open, with no cover. Orders were somehow delayed, but at 4.30 p.m. they were received - the Bridgehead over the Sadanawiyeh creek was to be taken. The 67th took up the task, and it consisted of an advance over 1,000 yards depth of flat open country, without support except that afforded by one machine gun from the other side of the river, and a Naval 3 pounder on a tug which had come up the river with the attack, in the face of heavy oblique, and almost enfilade, fire.

The Battalion advanced in two lines, on a 200 yards frontage, with 300 yards distance, sloped arms and fixed bayonets, while the machine gun and Naval gun rendered effective assistance in keeping down the enemy fire. The steady method in which this advance was conducted, shook the wavering morale of the Turks, and the advance continued up to the south bank of the creek. Here it was found that the Bridge had been completely destroyed. There was no means of crossing, and so there the Battalion had to remain for an hour, without support. The Turks however, had not the initiative to make an attack, and those in the direct front retreated, although those nearer the junction of the creek and the river, (the bridge had been some distance up the creek from the point of junction) kept up a heavy fire in the hope of inflicting casualties. Then the remainder of the Brigade came up on the left of the 67th, and it was ordered that the troops would bivouac on the ground for the night. The wounded were collected and sent to the river bank for transport, and the local boats with rations etc., were brought up. The attack on the right bank had prospered equally, and the 30th Brigade reached the level of the town, which had been evacuated, and, finding river craft on the spot, entered Nasiriyeh the same evening. The 12th Brigade bivouac was about 5 miles down stream of the town, and early on the 25th a bridge was thrown across the creek, and the 12th Brigade marched in to Nasiriyeh at 12.45 p.m., finding 4 abandoned enemy guns on the way. The day had been hot and trying during the attack on the 24th, particularly when the advance had to be through the humid air of palmgroves. The total casualties were 31 other ranks killed, 1 British Officer, 1 Indian Officer (Jemadar Khem Singh) and 34 Indian other ranks wounded. The Turkish casualties were estimated, from the combined attack, at 800 killed and wounded and 1,200 prisoners. On July 26th the Union Jack was formally hoisted over the Town. After the capture, the 30th Brigade were withdrawn, and the 12th Brigade left to garrison the town, and during August, both the wounded officers, Major Cox and Captain Atkins were able to rejoin the unit. In addition to local duties, the Battalion provided a detachment, under a British officer, at an important centre, Suk Es Shyuk, just upstream of the Hammar lake, when it was felt that the presence of a detachment might be of great political value. Although the victory at Nasiriyeh had a settling effect on the surrounding tribes, it could not be expected that such warlike men as the Muntifiks would become perfectly quiet at once, and their activities took the form of frequent sniping at such detachments. Many efforts were made under the direction, and even command, of British Officers, to ambush them but on no occasion did the peculiarly wily Arab bird come to the net spread for him! The Arab prowler and thief was in a very high class in that profession, and it was a much discussed point whether he was, or was not, superior to the transborder Pathan in India. Opinions differed, but it was generally conceded that the Arab had a slight advantage in the voting. At various times, it was necessary to send out punitive columns, either to repay active hostility or take measures against sniping at night; rarely was opposition met with. In time villages were held personally responsible for any sniping that could be traced to their locality, and this had the effect of reducing the sniping to NIL. During this period of comparative inactivity came the victory at Es-sinn Banks by the VI Division, and the capture of Kut-el-Amara, folfowed by General Townsend's advance on Baghdad, and the move of the Force Headquarters from Basra to Kut.

On October 10th the Regiment was ordered to Kurnah, and, crossing the Hammar lake in local boats, there being insufficient water for River steamers to be used, arrived at Kurnah on the 15th, being there joined by the Detachment from Suk. Orders came for the Regiment to proceed to Amara, which was reached on 23rd October, a detachment was dropped at Qalatsaleh, down the river en route on the 20th, and another sent to Ali elGharbi, up the river, the Headquarters remaining at Amarah.

Towards the end of November, the Regiment was once more united at Kut el Amara where was a supporting force to General Townsend's VIth Division, which had gone on in the hope of capturing Baghdad. On the 1st December 1915, half the Battalion was detailed for duty to form part of the escort to Sir John Nixon, the Army Commander, who had come up from Basra to be in closer touch with the Baghdad party. He was forced to return to Basra, as the ill fated force returned fighting to Kut, and a large escort had to be provided for this purpose. The escort wing under Captain Fenton, was thus parted from the Headquarters and remaining wing, under Bt.Lt.Col.C.E.S.Cox, and the two wings never joined again. The escort party formed the nucleus of the Regiment which was brought up to strength after the fall of Kut, and the rest were beseiged in Kut and finally taken prisoner. It is for the purpose of chronological accuracy that the beseiged part of the unit should now occupy by itself a space in the narrative, before proceeding to the further doings of the unit that succeeded it as a complete unit.

SKELETON MAP TO ILLUSTRATE SIEGE OF KUT AND FIGHTING ON THE SHUMRAN PENINSULA

CHAPTER VII

THE GREAT WAR - KUT-EL-AMARA

The history of General Townshend's ill-fated advance on Baghdad from Amara, which was undertaken as soon as the worst of the heat was passed, in mid September 1915, forms no part of the History of the 67th P. as they did not take part in it, but, as already stated, one half of the Battalion was caught in the trap at Kut El Amara. It is enough to say, here, that the final phase of the attack on Baghdad began on the 22nd November, when General Townshend's force was launched against Nuredin Pasha's main line defences, 18 miles from Baghdad, near the famous ruins of the Arch of Ctesiphon. In the attack, one British-Indian Division attacked 4 Turkish divisions, stormed their lines, wiped out one complete enemy division, and were then forced back to the Tigris by want of water. The position was impossible, and a retirement had to be made. This was done on the night of 30th Nov:/1st Dec., and was carried out successfully. On Dec: 3rd the pursuing Turkish army arrived within two hours' march of Kut, where General Townshend had taken up his position, and where he was beseiged. Among the troops then in Kut itself, was the remaining half battalion of the 67th Punjabis. This consisted of Nos: 2 & 3 D.Cs, and the following British officers.

```
Bt. Lt. Col: C. E. S. Cox.
Capt: M. C. Gribbon.
  "   R.F. Atkins.
  "   R. A. P. Grant  (112th Inf: Attd.)
Lt. F. G. S. McLean.
  "  F. H. C. Armstrong.
2nd Lt. H. H. Arbuthnott.
 "   "  A. F. Aldis  (I.A.R.O.)
```

Some days before the siege opened, there had been disturbing rumours that a large force of Turks were marching against Kut. It is probable that the basis of these rumours was the mixed force that molested the passage of the Army Commander on his departure downstream to Basra, which was rendered necessary by General Townshend's forced retirement on Kut. At the time that the VIth Division reached Kut, the garrison of that place was small, chiefly owing to the fact that all troops that could be spared, had been sent up to assist the attack on Baghdad. Food was prepared by the garrison in Kut, and sent out, on Dec: 2nd, for the use of the force retiring, and on the 3rd, the latter marched in, and preparations were at once started for putting the town in a proper state of defence. As soon as the investment of Kut was a known fact, measures for its relief were taken, by the organising and concentrating of a force down river, under General Aylmer V.C. General Townshend had the greatest confidence in himself and his troops, and looked forward to early relief, and therefore refused to entertain the Turkish Commander's summons to surrender. The main, and unceasing duty, of the beleaguered force, was forming their defensive works and communicating trenches, and, later during the siege, building high command trenches, which also afforded protection from flood, and fighting the percolation of water, and flood. And all engineers are agreed that the most difficult thing in the world to fight, is water. The confidence felt by the British General in his capacity to hold out until relief, was parallelled by that of the Turkish Commander in his power to reduce the place, and make the force surrender. His summons to surrender was actually delivered the day after the investment was completed, i.e. on Dec: 8th. On the previous day the shelling of the town was heavy, and it was on that day that the 67th P. had their first of the many casualties incurred, when Lt. McLean was hit by a bursting shrapnel, and he was unable to take further part in the defence throughout the siege. A reference to the sketch map will show that the river at Kut takes a "U" bend, and, on the E side, was a bridge to the right bank. On the evening of December 8th the 67th were detailed to send a Bridge head party, and this was provided by the men of the Regiment, with the M.G. Section, under the command of Capt. Gribbon. He reported his position as having been dug in, that evening. Shortly after dawn on the 9th, the Turks launched a heavy attack against this small position, and Capt. Gribbon was obliged to report his position as untenable. He therefore withdrew his small force to the left bank, suffering a number of casualties in doing so; but was ordered to recross, and re-occupy his former position. This he did, but was again forced to retire, and on this occasion suffered very heavily. He was himself mortally wounded. Lt. Arbuthnott, in endeavouring to bring in Capt. Gribbon, was badly wounded in the arm: Subedars Mahomed Din and Ahmed Khan were killed, as was also the Havildar of the M.G. Section,

Havildar Mahan Singh.   Further supports were called up, under Capt. Grant, and the original position was maintained, for the time, but the losses had been very heavy.   Orders were then given for the bridge to be destroyed, and this was effected.   Capt. Grant called for volunteers, and, during the night, crossed in a launch with some 20 men, in an attempt to bring in Capt. Gribbon's body.   On landing, they were fired at, from point blank range, and had to abandon their attempt, only returning with difficulty.   It was for this gallant attempt that Capt. Grant was awarded the M.C.   In Capt. Gribbon, the regiment lost a magnificent soldier, and a great gentleman.

The bombardment of Kut by the Turks continued with undiminished severity, and it was found that less casualties were caused by units remaining in the front line for a week at a time, instead of being relieved every 3rd day. The Turks' digging powers were amazing, and by Dec: 24th they had established themselves close up against the defences, some of their sapheads being less than 60 yards away.   In the meantime the Turks also launched attacks: the first on Dec: 12th, which was repulsed, and a further reply given by a counter attack of our troops holding the Liquorice Factory on the right bank, opposite the town, on the 14th.   Their communications being open, the Turks were enabled to send reinforcements to the investing force, and on Dec: 24th used a fresh Anatolian Division for the attack, made on the "Fort", - the main point of our front defence line, on its right flank.   For a time they succeeded in dislodging the garrison, but a fierce counter attack drove the enemy back, and the fort was regained - and held. Christmas day - a day that will never be forgotten by the defenders of Kut - brought no respite, attacks and counter attacks, fighting throughout the day, and well on in to the night.   On the 29th Muredin asked for an armistice to bury the dead, and remove the wounded, lying in numbers outside the 'Fort'.   This was granted.   At the end of the month, the garrison had lost 1,840 men, and the enemy losses were estimated at 4,000.   Some few days later, Lt. Arbuthnott returned to duty, and took over the M.G. Section, and one night decided to go outside the wire to improve the field of fire from a particular loop-hole.   In doing so, he was mortally wounded by a bullet that passed through his abdominal region, and out near the spine.   It was afterwards discovered that the bullet was a hollow-nosed large bore type, and the hollow had been fitted with a wooden plug.   He died a few hours after his getting to Hospital.

Finding his efforts to storm Kut abortive, Nuredin decided to close his investment more tightly, keep up bombardments at intervals, and wait for starvation among the garrison to come to his assistance. This rendered the life of the beleaguered troops less harassing, but their anxiety was increased by the doubts that began to creep in regarding the relief that had been so soon expected. News had come of their expected advance towards the end of December, and the sound of gunfire was heard with relief, on January 7th 1916. At this time the concentrated relief force were at Sheik Saad, some 25 miles down stream from Kut, a long way to traverse in face of a determined enemy to relieve an invested force. Enemy aircraft also began to appear, and began to bomb Kut during the 2nd week in February. In addition stores and supplies were decreasing, rations were cut down, and down, and scurvy began to add to the misery. The first effort of the relieving force, at Hannah, was broken by flood, on January 21st, and the same flood made the holding of the front line Kut defences impossible, as the river rose $10\frac{1}{2}$ feet. The troops were forced to withdraw to their "Middle line". The flood, however, dealt equally with both forces, and the Turks also had to withdraw their front lines, about 1200 yards. In doing so, they came within good mark of one of the redoubts, held to the last minute against the water, by the 67th, who were able to inflict a number of casualties before they also had to withdraw. The night of Jan: 21st was sheer misery. The O.C. Lt. Col: Cox was overcome, and had to be taken to Hospital - it was bitterly cold. Even the middle line trenches were, though to a less degree, flooded, but the day of the relief of the unit by another came on the 22nd, and that fact saved many a man from being sent to Hospital. Mens' hands and feet were swollen with cold and exposure, and in several cases, when a man took his boots off, he was unable to get them on again for some days. The British Officers were in no better plight. Two had been killed, four were in Hospital, and only Capt. Atkins and Lt. Armstrong were available for duty with the men.

With starvation stalking abroad, the same question arose in Kut, as arose at times elsewhere, that of the eating of 'unsanctified flesh'. Whether religious tenets in such a crisis should hold paramount importance, against the sheer necessity of keeping up physical strength, will always be a very difficult point among Orientals. In this case, the ultimate outcome could, as it turned out, not be affected by the stern religious ideas held by those involved, and the matter may be, therefore, left for academic discussion.

By the first week in February, the Indian ration was cut down to a small ration of atta, half ration of tea, and condiments, and a few dates. These, meagre as they were, had later to be still further reduced. In the second week of February the 67th P. went up again to the 'Fort', in relief of the Norfolks, and held the N.W. corner of the defence front line until the end of the seige. It was at this time that the enemy planes, commonly known as "Fritz", began their bombing, but without harm to the battalion, although Kut town suffered from the attention at various times. A 'Keep' was made in the Fort, in case it should be necessary to abandon the outer works owing to floods, but there was little activity from the Turks, except their frequent shelling. Sickness, however was taking a heavy toll, and it says much for the spirit of the men and officers that they were able to take an interest mingled with humour, in the enemy's doings with one particular "pompom". This was brought into use by the Turks, against the parties engaged in building the "Keep". Look-out men were able to give information when the "pompom" crew began to show signs of getting to business, when the fatigue parties would go to ground. After a burst of 7 or 8 rounds the pompom ceased work, and the fatigue parties resumed it.

On March 8th hopes were raised; from the direction of the awaited relieving force came sounds of heavy bombarding, but these hopes were dashed two days later when news came of the failure of the famous attack on the Dujailah Redoubt. On April 21st the attack on the Sannaiyat position seemed to seal the fate of Kut. It was now obvious to everyone, that, unless supplies could be got to the garrison, surrender must follow. One final attempt was made. The River steamer Julnar, stripped of all hamper, and loaded with stores of all kinds, was sent to try to break through the Turkish lines by river, to Kut. She was piloted by Capt. Cowley, probably the most experienced Captain on the River, assisted by an officer of the Royal Navy, and a first-class river crew. The initial arrangements were not sufficiently secret - news travels fast, and easily, - and from Arabs the Turks knew exactly what was happening. The attempt was doomed from the start, and the boat captured within sight of Kut. All efforts of the relieving force had equally failed, and on the night of the 26/27th April, the garrison of Kut began its work of destruction. All military stores were destroyed, and it was but an empty place, and a broken contingent, that the Turks took over on the 29th April, when the garrison, worn out with hunger and sickness, surrendered. Among the many in the unit whose lives were given up in Kut, it will bring a particular twinge of memory to those British officers, who knew him so well and for so many years, to recall the death of the Mess Havildar Lal Khan. He was accidentally killed by a bomb that exploded when he was carrying it, with others, down to the River to throw them in just before the surrender.

The history of the captured garrison, their toils, their trials, and their sufferings, have been recounted in many books, dealing with many places of internment, and all are records of subsequent poor treatment, varying in method and intensity. The following, however, taken from the record supplied by Capt. Atkins will be of interest to the readers of this narrative.

The incoming Turks despoiled the garrison of everything they could lay their hands upon - unless the owner had strength to keep them. The troops were marched 7 miles on the 30th April, and given hard, brown biscuits (of no nutritious value to a starving man, who was naturally unable to digest such stuff,) and several deaths resulted. Some of the stores from the Julnar were then brought up, and for a few days there was enough, but no restraint was placed on the wretched starving men, and further deaths were thus caused. On the 6th day, the march to captivity was begun, and British and Indian officers were sent by boat to Baghdad. Of the losses in Kut, there is no record available, but of the subsequent losses, on the march, and in camps of internment, it is estimated that among 2,500 surrendered British troops, only 450 survived to be released. The remaining British officers of the 67th - Lt. McLean was among the lucky ones who were sent, from various units, by Nuredin down to the British L. of C., after the fall of Kut - were sent to Kasta Mouni, in Asia Minor, 20 miles from the coast of the Black Sea. The first halt was, as stated, at Baghdad, where the inhabitants showed considerable sympathy, and where the first payments (to be deducted from the individual's subsequent pay as a Prisoner of War) were made. Thence, by train to

Samarra, where the British and Indian officers were separated. Thence the B.Os had to march, with very small allowance of kit, and poor transport, usually at night, to the first halt, at Mosul. The heartening news was there received, that officers were to be treated as honoured guests of the Turkish Govt: - soon found to be a mere hope, as there was no machinery to render such a promise effective! There was too much intrigue among the upper Turkish classes, and nothing was done to alleviate the conditions of the prisoners.

From Mosul, another week's march to Ras-el-Ain, where Indian orderlies were taken away from their officers. This was, possibly, part of a studied policy, to separate the British from their Indian troops at the start, and later try to get the Mahomedan troops to secede from their loyalty to the British Raj. From Ras-El-Ain the move to Aleppo was made in cattle trucks, and thence by road, rail, and motor to Kasta Mouni. Here these officers remained for 16 months when, owing to the escape of four among the prisoners, they were moved to Changri. During the 16 months at Kasta Mouni, the prisoners worked up from small beginnings to quite an amount of liberty. Games, and hobbies, such as carpentering, language study, shoe making, etc., and a good deal in the way of dramatic efforts. The worst part was the monotony, and the small annoyances continually caused by their 'keepers'. Officers, living from 2 to 8 in a room, had to provide everything for themselves, with but slight assistance from the authorities. After the move to Changri, where they remained for 2 months, the party was split up, and those who were prepared to give an undertaking not to try to escape, provided they were well housed, and given reasonable liberties, were sent to Kedos. Among these, went Lt. Col. Cox and Capt. Atkins, and it is a relief to find, from the records of the latter, that they met, in Kedos, a Turkish gentleman, in the person of their Camp Commandant "who would have been an ornament to any society in any country. He was a nature's gentleman, and a loyal Turkish subject, despite he realised his country's many shortcomings." Capt. Grant went to Yuzgad, where he joined the escape party, whose story is set down in "450 miles to Freedom"; while Lt. Armstrong was sent to Kara Hissak, after going for medical treatment to Constantinople. The peace with Turkey was signed on 28th October 1918, and on the 11th November, the day of the Armistice, the party from Kedos were in Smyrna awaiting repatriation. Their departure from Kedos had been hastened by a severe fire which broke out during one night, when theatricals were in progress. All the prisoners ran to the assistance of the local populace, where the English were particularly called upon by the women to help them save their household effects! Out of about 3,000 houses, only 200 to 300 were saved from the holocaust. From Smyrna the officers in due course arrived in England. It should be stated, that on the march to Kastamouni and onwards, Capt. Atkins was Staff officer to the senior British officer, and Lt. Armstrong acted in a similar capacity for a time at Kara Hissar. Capt. Atkins received a 'mention' for his services, and Lt. Armstrong was awarded the O.B.S.

CHAPTER VIII

MESOPOTAMIA AND ELSEWHERE

On the 2nd Dec: the escorting troops, moved out of Kut-el-Amara, and with some opposition the convoy proceeded downstream. On the 5th the force reached Ali Gharbi and the wing was ordered to take over that post on the 8th. This post now formed part of a series of posts that were brought into being, for the use of troops marching up from the base, so as to lighten the strain on the river Transport. These posts were semi-permanent, provided with defences, and defence troops, and capable of taking in the bodies of marching troops and transport. Life in these posts was relieved from monotony by the passing through of troops, and by the many duties that were required of the garrison; but it was not comparable to the former activities, snipers being the chief worry, but doing little damage. Thefts were fairly common at first, but the precautions taken were sufficient to render this amusement of the Arab, dangerous as well as difficult. On the 5th May 1916 the unit was relieved, and ordered to prepare, and occupy another new post, on the right bank of the river, downstream, which they reached on the 7th May, and named their new post Mudelil. A movable column was to be formed there, and would come under the command of Maj: W. R. B. Colan, 67th Punjabis. The movable column, consisting of small body of cavalry, 1 sec. R.F.A., and the 2 D.Cs of the unit made its first reconnaissance on May 20th the intervening period having been fully occupied in making the defences of the perimeter camp. The Battalion was also, at this period, receiving drafts and being made up to full unit strength again. Frequent parades of the movable column, with reconnaissances in the surrounding country, practice in crossing the Tigris etc., were held, and the efficiency of the unit was kept up to a high standard. It was found practicable at this post, to build a very fair rifle range, which was of great value in view of the large drafts that were arriving from India. At this place the unit remained, training, and practising the mobile column work, night work, and so on, until February 1917, when it received orders to move. This period of non-participation in active operations had been used to the best advantage, as the unit by this time was once more up to strength, and prepared for service. Life in the post was not by any means easy - living under tents in the hot season, even though the tents were further sheltered by "chappars", (thatched coverings on frames) was trying, and it says much for the spirit of all the ranks, that they were able to achieve the result of a well trained unit by the time that they were called upon for other duties elsewhere.

It is necessary, at this point, in order to follow the operations in which the Battalion subsequently took part, to realise what had been happening in the general outlook of the Campaign, since the fall of Kut. There can be no question that the failure in the Dardanelles, and the surrender of Kut, had results which were, politically, out of proportion to their military value. The results were felt both in Abyssinia, and in Persia. But it is noticeable that the fall of Kut did not lead to any offensive by the Turks against the two Divisions that had been so desperately struggling to relieve Kut. On the other hand, although the Turks must have been aware that as the result of continuous fighting against a heavily entrenched enemy, coupled with the attendant casualties, sickness, and exhaustion, the relieving troops must have reached the end of their resources, they retired! By the 20th May 1916, they had evacuated the right bank as far back as the Hai, which connects the Tigris and Euphrates from Kut to Nasiriyeh, only holding their bridges over the Hai, which was in flood and unfordable. This threw the onus of any offensive on to the British forces, and they were not going to face the trap. It was for the time being a stalemate, in the Mesopotamian Campaign. The Turks dare not move, and the British could not. But, as soon as the British move towards Baghdad had been stopped, and Kut fell, the Turks turned their attention to the Russians under General Baratoff, which had reached Karind, 150 miles N. of Baghdad. In the early Allied plan, it had been arranged that the Russian attack on Baghdad from the North, should synchronise with Townshend's advance from the East. With the British advance defeated, the Turks put large forces, some of them drawn from the force at Kut, in operation against

Baratoff, and drove him back from Karind, through Kermanshah, many miles within the Persian border, when he was able to stay the attack and save North Persia from being over run. In the meantime Sir Percy Sykes was employed on his magnificent march, making Southern Persia safe, and bringing in tribes to the British side, so reducing the elements of anarchy, and leaving friendship in his train. As part of the Home policy, the Mesopotamian Campaign was reorganised, and Sir Stanley Maude made Commander. New river steamers were brought into use, fresh aeroplanes, improved medical and supply arrangements, and a determined campaign evolved against sickness and insects; and, finally, the Railway was started. The floods were fought, and Basra, by means of wharves and jetties, was turned into a great seaport, with facilities for ocean-going steamers to load and unload. This wonderful reorganisation, carried out with rapidity and success, had a powerful effect on the Arab mind, and the news travelled far and wide in all directions throughout the East. The German leaders further assisted, by reducing the Turkish troops in Mesopotamia, for use in Galicia, and against the south eastern Russian army under Brussiloff, possibly in the mistaken idea that the British would not make any further effort, or that time would not permit them to make more than good after the disaster at Kut. Our seven months were spent in reorganising, gathering in reinforcements, and improving the situation generally.

By the second week in December, Gen. Maude was ready. Around Kut the Turks occupied some 30 miles of lines, along the bends of the Tigris. On the left bank, from the Suwaicha marsh to the river, on a narrow deep front; on the right bank the big defences of Es Sinn, to the Suwada marsh, on which rested their second fortified line. In the middle of December, the Hai was bridged and crossed, but the big objective in view was the bridge over the Tigris at the Shumran bend, and Gen: Maude hoped, not in vain, that his operations on the Hai would be regarded as a feint, designed to make the Turk reduce his strength on the left bank at Sinnaiyat. This was the conclusion reached by the Turkish Commander, and so he had his river communications raided by cavalry and aeroplanes for some miles above Kut. But in spite of fierce bombardment, attack in flank and even rear, the Turks held doggedly on, until the second week of January 1917, when he evacuated his position on the right bank, demolishing all works in the night of departure. But the British forces were not to be denied, and after days of desperate fighting around Kut, the mouth of the Hai was occupied by the British on February 3rd, the Turks retiring to the liquorice factory, whence their line stretched back to the Shumran Bridge. The factory was stormed and taken on the 10th, and the pressure increased the following days until the loop was in our hands up to Shumran. Still the Turkish Commander did not, or would not, realise that this was not just a feint to make him weaken the Sinnaiyat position. This was attacked on February 17th, but was not carried. Two lines were taken on the 22nd, and the Turk brought up reinforcements. The distance from his front to his rear, was 30 miles, and he was risking envelopment, if his rear was pierced in the Shumran bend. On Feb: 23rd, the main struggle opened, in the Shumran bend. As it was with these operations that the 67th Punjabis took their part, the narrative of the Battalion's work may now be continued from the time it was relieved from the river posts.

Orders were received on the 6th February 1917 for the posts occupied by the unit to be taken over by the 96th Infantry, and the Battalion was ordered to proceed up river to relieve the 36th Sikhs from the 37th Bde: of the XIV Division. This Division was located at the time in the vicinity of Kut, and was about to undertake to force a crossing over the Tigris, in face of heavy Turkish opposition, just upstream of the Town of Kut, where the river takes a big semi-circular bend, enclosing what was known as the Shumran Peninsular. Owing to heavy rain encountered on the last stages of the journey, which was completed by marching, great difficulty was experienced in getting the transport carts along, but eventually the unit took over from the 36th Sikhs, on the 18th February. A day was taken up in practising the method to be employed, of crossing, by ferries, on a tributary of the Tigris, and the operation proper was put into practice on the 23rd. The 37th Bde. was detailed to cover the crossing of the Division, and for its own crossing, was allotted

3 Ferries, one each to the Norfolk Regt:, the 2/9th Gurkha Rifles, and the 1/2nd Gurkha Rifles. The 67th Punjabis, being held in Reserve, were to cross, after the above three units, using all 3 ferries. The crossing met with such severe opposition, and so many of the rowers were incapacitated by enemy fire, that the 67th were finally allotted only one ferry of the original 3. The fact that this same ferry had to be used, for the same reason, by the two Gurkha Regiments as well, delayed the unit, and owing to heavy shelling by the enemy, ferrying was stopped after one company and Battalion Hdqrs: had crossed. The remainder crossed by the Bridge, completing the crossing at 5.30 p.m. The 37th Bde: then took up an outpost position to cover the Division behind them, and strong patrols were sent out, which located the enemy in force, some 300 yards beyond the piquet line. The casualties of the unit were small in the actual crossing, but 2 I.O.Rs were killed and 6 wounded. There was continued firing throughout the night, and the attack on the Dahra Ridge was ordered for 6.15 a.m. on the 24th, after a short bombardment. The 36th and 37th Bdes formed the attack, the 36th being on the right, with their left directing, so that the right of the 37th Bde was their directing flank. In the 37th Bde: the attack was led by the Norfolks on the right, and the 67th on the left, the latter being specially warned to clear the left flank, up to the river bank. The left flank was a cause of anxiety, as the fighting throughout was amongst buildings, all of which had to be cleared of snipers, and the lanes between the buildings were mostly swept by enemy machine gun fire. The first objective was a nullah held by the enemy in force, and as the attack proceeded, they launched a counter attack, which was repulsed with the aid of supporting troops, and Lewis guns. The attack proceeded, and the objective was captured. A further advance was made, and the 67th were finally held up by a very fierce fire from another hostile position. This again, was carried with the assistance of a company of the Buffs, from the 35th Bde, in support. Once more the advance was stopped, as all further approaches were held by enemy machine guns. The Battalion was then ordered not to incur further casualties, but to maintain positions occupied, and do everything possible to inflict loss on the enemy. In the meantime, other

troops had been moved round, under cover of the fighting, to try and take the enemy in rear. After dark the 67th were relieved. The casualties that had been sustained were heavy, 2 I.Os, (Sub: Gassandhar Singh, and Jem: Kala Khan) and 38 I.O.Rs killed: 5 B.Os (Capts. Colan, Riddell, and Bagnall, Lt. Hamilton and 2/ Lt. Curnow) 6 I.Os (Subs: Karam Dad Khan, Shakar Khan, and Baz Khan: Jems: Ghulem Khan, Sharif Khan, and Khushia) and 154 I.O.Rs. wounded. The enemy were dispersed and retreated. The general situation was as follows. After the Shumran attack had proved successful the Turks had no option but to retire: they were taken in rear, and would be enveloped. They blew up their magazines, on their way back from the front positions, 30 miles away, and as they retreated the British gunboats followed up, decks clear for action, taking on the role of pursuing cavalry. Kut was once more in our hands, and the Turks were retreating hard on Baghdad, rapidly followed by the victorious force. The Turks had a depot farther up river, at a place called Baghaila, and it was obvious from the strenuous efforts they made to collect and fight a rear-guard action, that they hoped to stave off pursuit long enough to enable them to clear the guns and stores from this depot to Baghdad. However, on February 25th this last rearguard was enveloped and dispersed. Although, between Feb: 24th and Feb: 27th only 4,300 prisoners were taken, the defeat round Kut, and the subsequent retreat, were a very severe blow. Their losses were put at about 30,000 and these were largely picked troops from Gallipoli, and those who had beaten Townshend back to Kut. When they went, only a mob remained, and this mob, on the evening of Feb: 27th passed through Azizie, on the left bank of the Tigris, 55 miles from Kut and 45 from Baghdad. The pursuit continued, the last effort made by the Turks being at Laj, 25 miles from Baghdad, from which they were driven. On March 6th, the force under Gen: Maude arrived at the farthest point that had been reached by Gen: Townshend, Ctesiphon. The fall of Kut reacted on the Turkish forces in Northern Persia, and they also retired, followed up in pursuit by Gen: Baratoff, who recovered the hold on Kermanshah. This left the Russian force 167 miles from Baghdad, and the British only 14. The Turkish force could offer no resistance to the oncoming Russians, for fear of having their communications cut by the

British, on the North of Baghdad. The Turks retiring in front of Gen: Maude were in no better position, and both Turkish forces hoped for reinforcements to arrive from Mosul and avert the fall of Baghdad. In the retirement of the Southern Turkish force, they crossed the Diala river, and destroyed the bridge.

Our operations against Baghdad opened on March 7th. The method to be employed was that of a double movement, similar to that employed against Kut. One force to make an enveloping attack from the South-West, while a frontal attack was organised from the line of the Diala. To return to the 67th. After the XIIIth Division had followed up the Turks, in the direction of Sheik Jaad, the Battalion was left to clear up the battlefield, and was, on Feb: 28th ordered to rejoin its Division. This was done on March 3rd, at Azizie. Thence the advance of the XIIIth and XIVth Divisions was carried forward to the Diala, when the Battalion, with the 37th Bde:, encamped on March 10th. The Diala river runs North and South, to the junction with the Tigris, and on the 10th March, the 37th Bde: crossed from the left bank, without opposition; the 67th forming the covering party. Owing to heavy winds, the crossing by boats was much hampered, but was finally accomplished, and the Bde: concentrated on the 11th, on the right bank.

On this same day, the enveloping movement achieved its object, and the Union Jack was hoisted over Baghdad. The Turkish force retreating before this British success, moved Northwards, in an endeavour to join with the other force retreating from Persia, with a view to a combined action southwards, against our troops on the Diala.

On the night 13/14th Lt. Col: Colan was assigned a task by the Hd: Qrs: XIVth Division. He was placed in command of a force consisting of 240 of the 67th, one Section No: 187 M.G.Co:, one Section of S. & M., with pack wireless, and Medical details. His orders were to proceed to Baqubah, 35 miles up the Diala, to gain possession of the bridge of boats, and of a store of grain reported there, and secondly to establish a defensive post. This force was transported in Ford motor vans, (whence it got the name of the "Motor raid") and left on the 14th, arriving the same evening at Baqubah, without meeting opposition. It was found that the bridge had been demolished, and local information stated that 1500 enemy, with guns, were holding Baqubah on the left bank: the right bank was clear. Shortly after midnight the remainder of the 67th were ordered to join the force, which they did on the 15th. In the meantime, (there was no bridge), Colan had been unable to find any boats to assist a crossing, and the enemy had been shelling and firing from the other bank, where they were hidden in buildings, and date groves, where they could not be located. Colan's force was without transport, except it's Ford vans, and unable to cross. Two Havildars of the 67th, Ali Ahmed, and Harbans did succeed, gallantly, in securing two boats from the further bank, under enemy fire, but that was not sufficient to allow of any attempt to make a crossing in face of the enemy.

The situation being reported to Divisional Hd: Qrs:, further action was taken.

Br: Gen: Edwardes was sent with another force the following day. His instructions were for Colan's force to make a demonstration of crossing the river 4 miles North of Baqubah, while his own force would effect a crossing a few miles South of the town. This operation was duly carried out, and the demonstration above, and crossing below effected. Two Battalions of Br: Gen: Edwardes' force crossed, and, moving up the left bank, entered Baqubah unopposed.

The case of further assistance being needed, Br: Gen: Keary was also sent, with another column, and crossed at the same point as Br: Gen: Edwardes had done, and was shortly afterwards withdrawn.

The 67th then crossed, to a bivouac position on the North of the town, leaving a company to guard the bridgehead on the right bank. The town was taken over by the 37th Bde: on the 23rd March.

Certain movements of units, and other arrangements were made, so that the troops at Baqubah could render, if required, assistance to others in the vicinity; but as they were not called upon for this, they were employed in constructing the defences of Baqubah.

Detachments were sent out to neighbouring points, but no active operations were undertaken, and the Battalion returned as a whole, to Baqubah on May 27th, resuming the defensive duties previously undertaken. During the period of these operations near Baqubah, local tribes, - not being sure which way the pendulum might swing, and ever ready to create trouble if there was a chance of their own advantage accruing therefrom, - had been getting difficult, and it was found necessary to take steps against them. On June 2nd, therefore, a column was formed under command of Br: Gen: Maclachlan to undertake punitive measures. The column consisted of the 67th, the 2/9th G.R., one Squadron Indian Cavalry, one Section R.F.A., one section M.G.Coy, with pack wireless, and medical details. Two Light Armoured cars were also provided to co-operate. The punitive measures took the form of burning hostile villages, and - more serious still to the inhabitants - taking away all available live stock. The terrain of operations was the stretch of country between Baqubah and Beled Ruz, some 25 miles East of the former place. Their mission being duly accomplished, with the rounding up of camels, cattle, and sheep, and the destruction of several villages, and meeting no serious opposition, the column returned to Baqubah on June 7th. But it was found necessary to send another column on the 22nd June, to the same neighbourhood, and that column was kept at Beledruz for a considerable period. There was no active hostility, and the 67th, which formed part of the column, settled down to defence works, training, and at times moving out on reconnaissance duties in the surrounding country.

On June 28th 2nd Lt. H. Graham, of the 74th Punjabis, (attached to 67th), volunteered to go out, in charge of a cavalry patrol, in the direction North West of the village. During this duty, the patrol became heavily engaged with some 200 Arabs, mostly mounted, and in withdrawing the patrol, Graham, and four of the 32nd Lancers were killed. Their bodies were never recovered.

Signs of trouble, further North, in the Jebel Hamrin hills, were forming, and on August 18th a force was moved out to reconnoitre in that direction. It was found that the hills were held by the Turks, and as the force was not sufficiently strong to go forward, it was withdrawn to Beledruz on August 21st.

In this place the 67th remained, at normal duty, until the middle of October 1917.

On October 13th, a secret memorandum was received, with the information that the 37th Bde:, with attached troops, would shortly be moving on operations. These operations were with the object of turning the Turks out of the Jebel Hamrin hills, and, further, of securing control of the canal system up the Diala, North of Baqubah. The Turks did not offer resistance to this advance, but, finding that it was quite possible for their retreat westward to be cut off, if the advance made a turning movement, they left their positions on the hills, and effected the retreat, over the Diala. The advance, however continued, and succeeded in turning the Turks out of their further Northern positions at Qizil Robat, in spite of the firing kept up by the first retreating force, from the right bank of the river. In this operation the Turks showed no initiative, and appeared to be too demoralised to take advantages of the opportunities that they had.

It was during these operations, when the 67th were in camp at Kurdarrah crossing, on October 31st, that two British aeroplanes, (which had been sent out to search for two other missing aeroplanes,) made a forced landing, two miles beyond the outpost line, part of which was held by the 67th. The Turks immediately opened fire on these two 'planes, and then Maj: H.N. Colan D.S.O., accompanied by Lt. E. Curnow and Lt. H.J. Hannah, collected a party of men who were working on the outpost line at the time, and went out to the assistance of the airmen. In spite of the Turkish shelling, they succeeded in bringing the aeroplanes and personnel safely through the outposts. For this fine achievement they received the thanks and appreciation of the Bde: and Divisional Commanders, the former of whom had been a witness of the incident.

The month of November was quiet, save for desultory and ineffectual bombing by enemy aircraft, but on the 25th of that month, a secret memorandum was received from the 37th Bde: to the effect that mobile operations might be undertaken shortly. In order that these might be put into force, it was necessary to find a ford over the Diala, and reconnoitring parties, under British Officers were sent out to try and discover the required ford. These patrols were used at night, to avoid the possibility of enemy observation, and for some nights the search was unsuccessful, but a ford was finally found on Dec: 2nd, with a strong current, and a depth of about 4 feet. Finally a ford of about $2\frac{1}{2}$ feet was found, and this was used. This, however, was not the finish, as two more branches of the river were later discovered, which also had to be forded. The second branch was the deepest, and had the strongest current, but all three were negotiated successfully, and the advance was continued, the 67th being on the left, with the 2/9th G.R. on their right, with cavalry on the right flank. Although the Turks had placed ranging marks in front of their position, the advance on December 3rd seemed to shake their morale, as they did not succeed in causing any casualties. They preferred to get cover in nullahs, and retire. The Turkish artillery kept up a regular fire, but that also appeared to be of no effect. The advance was steadily continued, mainly over cultivated ground which the Turks had flooded, and thus rendered the "going" difficult, the objective being the village of Telburdan. This was reached, without any casualties, at 3.15 p.m. that afternoon.

Although no casualties were suffered it is worthy to record the actual work carried out by the troops engaged on that day. The advance commenced at 3.15 a.m. on the 3rd December, and by the time the objective was reached 12 hours later, the Battalion had covered nearly 25 miles, which including the fording of the three branches of the Diala, and that, in face of the enemy. It is easily understood that, with their clothing still wet, carrying only greatcoats, and no other covering, the officers and men got very little sleep in the cold air at that time of the year.

The 35th Bde: had moved by another route on the same objective, and the two Bdes: came into touch as intended.

The Turks had retired beyond touch, and the active operations then ceased.

On December 9th, the Battalion moved to Ruz, where it remained until Feb: 6th, when it went to Kurdarrah, and was there employed in defence works, and on the construction of the Kurdarrah-Quizil Robat road. This duty provided the Battalion with a knowledge of the various stages in road construction, and was carried out in addition to other duties. On March 24th the Battalion went to Tawilah carrying on the road work, and also the start of the embankment for the projected Railway. It was during this period, and subsequently, that the Battalion was called upon to provide considerable drafts for one of the new units being formed, namely, the 2/152nd Indian Infantry.

The work done by the Battalion on the Tawilah position, and the Railway construction was the subject of a commendatory letter from the G.O.C. XIVth Division, fully endorsed by the 37th Bde: Commander. The unit remained at work at Tawilah, until Sept. 5th, and several officers were able to avail themselves of short leave to India, during this period. On the 5th Sept: the Regt. moved up to Marjanah where they continued training, and also providing detachments, and from here sent several officers and men for duty and training in specialist subjects to Baghdad. On October 1st, in accordance with secret orders previously received, that the unit had been selected to proceed to another sphere of operations, it returned to Ruz and entrained on the 6th taking boat transport on the 7th from Kut-el-Amara, arriving Basra on Oct: 10th, and embarked, changing ship at Fao on the 16th October, and disembarking at Port Said on Nov: 2nd. On Nov: 11th they embarked for Salonika, arriving there on the 19th, and remained, training until orders were received for the unit to embark on February 16th 1919. Disembarked at Batoum on Feb: 21st, and marched to billets. The next move was to Tiflis on April 20th where they were employed in local duties, with detachments, until moved to Gori on June 12th, from which place a detachment was provided for special escort duty to Tabriz. The unit returned to Tiflis on July 4th. During this month the unit provided guards and duties, and detachments, including a Guard of Honour for the Shah of Persia, and also another for the British High Commissioner for Caucasus. For the latter, a letter of congratulation on the smartness and turn out of the guard was received, as was also a letter from the G.O.C. British Troops in the Caucasus, appreciating the work done by the Battalion in Tiflis. From there the unit entrained for Batum on Sept: 8th, arriving on the 10th. They remained there until February 1920, when it moved to Chanak (Dardanelles). Here they were employed in constructing defences round the town, and in May 1920, provided covering parties for the Royal Navy, in their work of destroying all the old Turkish guns in the surrounding Forts. On September 13th the Battalion embarked for India, arriving in Bombay on October 1st 1920. The Battalion has thus spent 5½ years out of India.

The following Table shows the casualties of the Battalion, 1914-1920:-

Theatre	Killed, died of disease etc.			
	B.Os	I.Os	N.C.Os & Sepoys	Followers
Force "A" (France) Captain R. Reed	1	-	-	-
N.W.F. 1915 - 18	-	2	1	-
N.W.F. 1919 - 20	-	-	1	-
Mesopotamia Force "D" ˣCaptain M.C.Gribbon Lieut. H.H.Arbuthnott 2/Lieut. C. Aldis " H. Graham	4ˣ	6	162	6
Salonika Expeditionary	-	-	7	-
Total	5	8	171	6
	Wounded			
Force "A" (France)	-	-	-	-
N.W.F. 1915 - 18	1	1	-	-
N.W.F. 1919 - 20	-	-	-	-
Mesopotamia Force "D"	11	7	186	2
Salonika Expeditionary	-	-	-	-
Total	12	8	186	2

CHAPTER IX

BACK IN INDIA

The depot of the Battalion while on service was at Agra, and on return to India, the Battalion proceeded there, arriving on October 3rd. All men who had been on service were sent forthwith on 2 months leave. The combined strength of the returned unit, and the depot, was well above the normal establishment, and orders were received for reduction to establishment of 826, within 4 months of the date of arrival in Bombay. By the 31st January 1921, the necessary demobilization had been completed, and on February 2nd the unit was moved to Nowshera, where it remained 8 months.

In May 1921, many changes in composition were introduced into the Indian Regiments, but the only change affecting the 67th was the replacement of Dogra Rajputs, and Dogra Brahmins, by Dogra Jats. It can be well understood that during the months following their return to India, the unit was in a state of constant change. The elasticity in recruiting, authorised to meet the requirements of manpower for the needs of War, had caused an inflow of many men of castes that were normally not recruited into the Army during peace: these had to be in due course, returned whence they came, and the correct classes authorised for the unit recruited in their place. On 28th September the Battalion moved to Peshawar, and in March 1922 the Battalion took their part in lining of the route for the visit of H.R.H. the Prince of Wales, and also, on his arrival, provided a Guard of Honour at the residence of the Chief Commissioner. On the 1st March, also, the new grouping system came into being, as has been noted elsewhere, and the 67th, with their two former links, the 69th and 74th, with the 72nd and 87th Punjabis, formed the 2nd I.I.Group, with the 2/67th Punjabis forming the Training Battalion. Under this scheme in December 1922, the 67th Punjabis were re-named the 1/2nd Punjab Regiment, and the 2/67th became the 10th/2nd Punjab Regiment, all Training Battalions being given the number 10 in their respective groups. During 1922 many officers were retired under the Royal Warrant of April 1922, the Battalion losing 10 in all. In 1923 a new order was issued regarding terms of service under which an Indian Infantry soldier had to serve for not less than 5 years in army service, with a liability to serve in the

Reserve, for a further period sufficient to complete a total period of 15 years. Certain specified "special recruitments" such as Bandsmen, Buglers, Drummers, Schoolmasters, Clerks, and others, had to serve for 10 years army service. Special conditions were also laid down regarding procedure in the case of men who had enlisted under the previous terms of service and were desirous of coming under the new terms. The Reserve was divided into two classes, according to length of army service, and at the end of a total 15 years army and Reserve service a man was discharged. In the same year the establishment was reduced from 826 to 762 Indian Ranks.

In February 1924 the Battalion moved to Khirgi, in Waziristan, when they were employed in furnishing Camp Perimeter Piquets and road protection duties. There were several raiding parties reported, and on 27th March, a company of the Battalion under Major Atkins and Captain Harwood was despatched to the assistance of a company of the 2/3rd Sikh Pioneers, and enabled the latter to get away, with their casualties, when Major Atkins also retired his company, closely followed by the raiders, but no casualties were suffered. Throughout this period "sweeps" were commonly used to disperse raiding parties, the Battalion doing its full share of this work. On May 15th the Battalion (less 2 Coys. left at Khirgi) moved to Manzai, and was joined by the Khirgi detachment on 11th October. On November 10th the Battalion moved to Sararogha, in connection with the Razmak Road project, and was employed on movable column, piquet, and bridge construction duties.

Further alterations in class composition took place in 1925, Dogra Rajputs and Kanets being brought in. In this year, the grant of the Indian General Service Medal was made to all troops who had served in Waziristan between December 21st 1921 and March 31st 1924, or a clasp to those already in possession of the medal.

On May 29th 1925, the Battalion moved to Tank, providing various detachments from there. Under the programme for reliefs for 1925-1926, the Battalion was detailed for Ahmadnagar. In order to permit the troops to avail themselves of the sanctioned 3½ months' leave on completion of a tour of duty in Waziristan, half the Battalion proceeded direct from Tank and rejoined at Ahmadnagar in June 1926, while the H..Q. and remainder moved to Ahmadnagar on Feb: 23rd, arriving at their destination on February 28th, 1926.

At the time of closing this history, the Battalion is still stationed at Ahmadnagar.

Casualties among British Officers, not serving with the Battalion at the time

During the operations against the Mohmand tribe in 1908, Lieut. W. Young, 67th Punjabis died at Galanai on May 30th 1908, from wounds received at Khuda Khel on the previous day.

In 1915, Captain T. Reed, 67th Punjabis, was serving in France, with the 59th Rifles. F.F. This Battalion formed part of the Sirhind Brigade, and the Brigade took part in an attack on the Bois Du Biez on the morning of March 12th, this attack being a part of the operations that were known as the Battle of Neuve Chapelle. While Captain Reed was bringing up the Machine gun section of the Battalion, he was killed.

CHAPTER X

THE 2/67th PUNJABIS

When the 1/67th Punjabis proceeded on Field Service in March 1915, the 2/67th Punjabis was formed as a provisional Battalion, for the period of the War, at Loralai. This Battalion consisted of all details of the 1/67th left at Loralai, Reservists of the 67th, 69th, and 74th, and one Company from the 66th. But, owing to the calls for men entailed by the War, no limit was placed on the caste of men recruited, nor on the District from which they came. The main duty of the Battalion was the training of recruits, and the furnishing of drafts to the 1/67th and other units, as required. During 1915, 1916, and 1917, the total enlistments numbered 1521.

The Battalion moved from Loralai to Tank, arriving there on April 4th 1917. On April 18th the Battalion marched to Khajuri Kach, leaving half the Battalion at Nilikach post.

On May 1st, when this half Battalion was en route to join Headquarters at Khajuri Kach, in company with the piquetting troops of the 94th Infantry, they were ambushed by Mahsuds in the Nili Nullah, about 5 miles from Nili Kach. In this ambush Capt. G.G.Everett, Subedar Mit Singh, Jemadar Tahil Singh and 25 rank and file were killed. 2/lt. R.L. Frost, Jemadar Dasaundi Ram and 25 rank and file were wounded. The half Battalion and the piquetting troops then returned to Nili Kach.

On May 7th 1917, the Waziristan Field Force came into being, and the Battalion was employed in garrisoning the two posts it already occupied, on the L. of C. to Wano. On relief in July 1917, the Battalion moved to Tank, forming part of the garrison at that place.

In December 1918, the Battalion moved to Rawalpindi, and to Chaklala in March 1919. On May 7th, it was ordered to mobilise for service against Afghanistan, and moved to Nowshera, arriving there on the 9th. On relief, moved to Peshawar arriving there on the 23rd.

The Battalion was then employed moving up to Jamrud and then Ali Masjid, on escort duty, and subsequently taking over various forts, supplying escorts and piquotting troops. At the beginning of July, the Battalion was relieved of the upper forts, and took over the lower Khyber posts of Bagiari, Fort Mande, and Shagai, with their subsidiary road piquets.

On July 18th, one of these piquets, named Barlem Hill, which was subsidiary to, and about 1200 yds. distant from Fort Mande, was attacked by 500 to 600 Bazar valley tribesmen. Fort Mande was under command of Lt. (Actg: Capt.) A. Oates, D.S.O., who gave able assistance with long range fire, and by sending reinforcements ammunition etc, and helping in every possible way. The piquet was finally rushed when all ammunition had been expended. Jemadar Hussain Shah was killed with the piquet. Lt. Oates received the M.C. for his gallantry, and Subedar Allah Dad Khan the Indian Order of Merit for his bravery when sent out in charge of reinforcements. One Havildar in the piquet gained the I.D.S.M. and three sepoys the I.O.M. 2nd class. Artillery fire saved the defeated piquet from being captured, and drove the enemy away. Commendatory notes were received from the Divisional, and Force Headquarters.

On August 30th the Battalion took over the upper posts, in addition to the lower, until relieved and returning to Ali Masjid on September 9th. There the Battalion remained until 1st September 1920, when it followed its Depot, sent the previous year, to Agra.

In March 1921, the Battalion was sent to Mesopotamia, returning to India, and arriving in Multan on 1st October 1921.

On March 1st, 1922, this Battalion was formed into the Training Battalion for the 2nd Indian Infantry group, which consisted of the 1/67th, 69th, 72th, and 87th Punjabis.

The requisite reorganisation of all these units, to bring them once more back to their authorised classes etc, was the cause of the 2/67th having to enlist a large number of extra recruits, in order to make up the deficiencies in the Battalions of the group.

On taking over the duty of a Training Battalion, the 2/67th Punjabis ceased as a unit, and, when the re-numbering was carried out on December 2nd, 1922, it became the 10th Battalion 2nd Punjab Regiment.

APPENDIX A

Badges and Devices

1.   7th Madras Infantry - 1880.

Helmet ornament, in silver for British officers, consisting of the numeral "7" in the centre of a garter, with the word "Ava" inscribed on the upper curve of the latter, the whole being surmounted by a crown.   To be worn on a grounding of cloth, of the colour of the facings of the Regiment, brooched on to the turband.

(A.G. in India No.619 of 3. 3. 1880)

2. 7th Madras Infantry - 1884.

Forage Cap Badge. The numeral "7" within a plain circle. Surmounted by a crown: folded within two wings of a laurel wreath. The word Ava at centre of lowest part of the laurel wreath. The numeral on a red background.

(A.G. in India No: 1361 of 5. 5. 1884)

3. 7th Madras Infantry. 1892.

Regimental Badge. The numeral "7" on yellow background, in the centre of a garter, the latter inscribed "Carnatic" "Ava" "Mysore" from left to right, in that order. The garter surmounted by a crown, and enclosed by a laurel wreath.

(A.G. in India No: BA/713 d/25. 3. 1892)

4. 7th Madras Infantry (reinstituted) 1902.

To use the Badges and devices of the old Battalion, namely "Carnatic" "Mysore" and "Ava".

(G.G.O. No: 828 of 1902)

5. 67th Punjabis 1903.

Consequent on the renumbering, the following changes were made in Badges.

Forage cap. Badge in metal, a "67" encircled by a Sikh Quoit with a crescent below, on which was inscribed "Punjabis". Underneath, a scroll bearing the words "Carnatic" "Ava" "Mysore". The whole surmounted by a Tudor Crown, with ten pearls on either side of the arch of the cross.

(A.G. in India No: 3807 B. d/ 20. 11. 1903)

6.   2nd Punjab Regt: 1926.

Badges for 1st 2nd 3rd 5th and 10th Battalions

on Collar of tunic and Mess jacket

    A galley in gold braid.

On Forage Cap

    A galley in gold braid.

On Service dress cap

    A bronze galley with a scroll below inscribed "2nd Punjab Regt"

    (G. of I. Notification No: 790 d/ 18. 6. 1926)

APPENDIX B.

Detail of Battle Honours, giving the authority for their use

1. (G.O. No: 84 d/ April 11th 1826)

    In testimony of the brilliant services achieved by the Army under the command of Maj: Gen: Sir Archibald Campbell, the Governor General in Council is pleased to resolve that all corps, European and Native, in the service of the Honourable East India Company, who have been employed in the Burman country for the conquest of the Enemy's possessions of .... - Tavoy and Mergui......... shall bear on their Regimental colours the word

    " A V A "

2. (G. O. C. No: 250 of 3rd May 1889)

    On the 26th April 1889, Her Majesty the Queen Empress of India has graciously sanctioned the undernoted words being inscribed on the colors and appointments of the 7th Regiment, M.A., in commemoration of it's services during the campaigns in the Carnatic and Mysore in 1780-84, and 1790-92.

        1st.   For services during the Campaign of 1780-84 the word

    " CARNATIC "

        III   For services during the Campaigns in Mysore in 1790-92, the word

    " MYSORE "

3. Gazette of India Notification No: 193 dated February 20th, 1926

    No:193 His Majesty the King has been graciously pleased to approve of the undermentioned units of the Indian Army bearing the distinction

    "AFGHANISTAN. 1919"

upon the standards, Regimental Colours, and appointments respectively, in recognition of their services during the Campaign known as the " 3rd Afghan War".

....
2nd Punjab Regiment.

4. Gazette of India Notification No: 194 dated February 20th 1926.

No: 194. His Majesty the King has been graciously pleased to approve of the grant to Regiments of the Indian Army and Indian State Forces of the following Battle Honours in recognition of their services in campaigns during the Great War (1914-18).

The Battle Honours which have been selected to be borne on colours or appointments, are printed in heavy type.
....
2nd Punjab Regiment
.....

"<u>Loos</u>". "France and Flanders 1915" "<u>Helles</u>" "Krithia" "<u>Gallipoli 1915</u>" "Suez Canal" "Egypt <u>1915</u>" "Megiddo" "Sharon" "Nablus" "<u>Palestine 1918</u>" "Aden" "<u>Defence of Kut-Al-Amara</u>" "Kut-Al-Amara 1917" "<u>Baghdad</u>" "<u>Mesopot-1915-1918</u>" "North West Frontier, India 1915, 1916-17".

(In place of heavy type underlining has been used)

APPENDIX C.

List of Commandants, as far as shown in available records

Year	Rank and Name	Year	Rank & Name
1761	Capt. Cooke	1854	Lt.Col. C.A.Browne
1789	Capt. R. Chase	1855	" C.Wahab
1793-5	Capt. T. Bowser	1856	Bt.Col. R.Thorpe
1801-4	Lt. Col. A. Lindsay	1857	" J.Davidson
1805-6	Lt. Col. C. Godfrey	1858	Lt.Col. S.A.Duke
1807-8	" E. O. Reilly	1859	" W. Reece
1810	" I. G. Graham	1860-1	Bt.Col. W. Reece
1811-12	" T. Wilson	1863-4	" D.Babbington
1813	" N. Forbes	1865	Lt.Col. W.T.Money
1814-15	" T. Wilson	1866-7	" T.J.Batten
1816-17	" J. U. Symons	1868	" F.F.Warden
1818	" Prendergast	1869-72	Bt.Col. R.Woolley
1820-23	" R.McDowall	1873-4	Col. E.W.Boudier
1824	" E. Chitty	1875	Col. T.J.H.Keyes
1826-8	" T. H. Smith	1876-7	" G.T.Hilliard
1829-32	" H. Bowdler	1878-9	" G.H.Johnstone
1833-4	" S. Townsend	1880-3	" T.A.Baldwin
1835	" T. King	1884	" W.H.G.Palmer
1836	" J. Bell	1885-7	" N.Swanston
1837-40	" H. Walpole	1889	" C.Hayter C.B.
1841-2	" W. N. Burns	1889-91	Lt.Col. A.J.Shaw
1843-5	" J. D. Stokes	1892	Col. G.Simpson
1846	" T. M. Cameron	1893-) 1900)	Capt. G.P.M. Prichard (later Lt. Col.)
1847-52	" C. W. Nepean		
1853	Bt.Col. W. Instice	1901	Lt.Col. D.S.Lewis

After re-organisation as a Punjab Battalion

1902

Rank and Name	Period	
Bt. Col. G.W. Maxwell	15. 11. 02 to	29.2. 08
Col. A.W. Newbold	1. 3. 08 "	28.2. 13
Lt. Col. H.W. Johnston	1. 3. 13 "	20.11.17
" W.R.B.Colan, D.S.O.	21.11.17 "	20.11.21
" H.R.E.Pratt, D.S.O.	1. 4.22 "	31. 3.24
" H. Greenaway	5 4.24 "	4. 4.28
" A. Riddell, D.S.O.	5 4.28 "	date

APPENDIX D

Nominal Roll of Officers who belonged to the Battalion between 1902 and 1928

(This list does not include Commandants shown elsewhere)

- x A. V. Alexander
- x C. E. S. Cox
- x E. Dickson
- x N. Ogle, D.S.O.
- x H. M. Colan, D.S.O.
- x R. F. Atkins
-    G. L. Carter
-    H. A. Scott
-    A. N. Davidson
-    A. L. Watson
- x T. Luck
- x A. H. Burnett, D.S.O.
- x F. G. S. McLean
-    M. Middleton
-    H. T. Craig
- x J. D. Scale, D.S.O., O.B.E.
- x E. W. Morris, D.S.O.
- x A. H. Crowther
-    G. R. Clarke
- x E. L. Harrison
- x G. J. E. Manisty
-    W. St. G. Chamier
- x N. M. Geoghegan
-    H. P. Watts
- x T. G. J. Torrie
- x D. R. G. Oliver
-    T. S. Johnson

- x M. C. Gribbon
- x H. S. Tyndall
- x W. C. Hutcheson
- x A. S. Clark
-    A. G. Williamson
- x W. B. C. Higgs
- x T. Reed
- x A. D. Martin
- x G. G. Everett
- x J. de la H. Gordon
- x A. C. S. Palin
- x F. H. C. Armstrong
- x W. D. Churcher
- x H. H. Arbuthnott
- x G. C. Ballentine
- x A. J. Hannah
- x C. O. Crawford, M.C.
-    F. A. Latter
- x F. G. Mc Caughey
-    D. Moriarty
-    G. E. Harwood
- x K. T. Stephens, M.C.
- x C. C. Deakin
-    E. Byers
-    C. D. Clapp
- x A. W. S. Mallaby
-    A. Whiteside

   Masud Hayat

As far as available records show, Officers marked 'x' served in the Great War, either with the Battalion, or elsewhere.

APPENDIX E

Nominal Roll of Attached Officers, who served with the Battalion during the Great War.

- E. Curnow.
- J. M. Mathews.
- F. J. Ashton.
- A. R. S. Hayne.
- L. S. Fenton.
- C. B. Sexton.
- R. Bagnall.
- J. L. Longbottom.
- V. H. Raynor.
- A. F. Aldis.
- A. V. Nash.
- O. P. Hamilton.
- R. N. Cable.
- R. A. P. Grant.
- H. Graham.
- H. C. Prescott.
- A. G. Crawford.
- A. H. Harper.
- H. B. Yorke.
- W. G. Wolstonholme.
- S. G. Lane.
- J. Murray.
- A. Dyson.
- J. W. Dippie.
- H. N. Hayle.
- J. B. Chapman.
- C. Drysdale.
- T. W. Meneer.

APPENDIX F

List of Honours and Awards granted 1915 - 1920

Distinguished Service Order

    Lt. Col. W. R. B. Colan.
    Bt. Lt. Col. N. Ogle.
    Major H. N. Colan.
    Major A. Riddell. (74th attd. 67th)

Brevet Rank

    Major C. E. S. Cox, to be Bt. Lt. Col.
    Major N. Ogle   " " " " "

Order of the British Empire

    Capt. F. H. C. Armstrong, O.B.E.

Order of St. Stanislas. (Russian)

    Lt. Col. W. R. B. Colan, D.S.O.

Italian Silver Medal "Al merito di Guerra".

    Major R. Bagnall (74th attd. 67th)
    Capt. E. Curnow.

Honorary King's Commission as Lieutenant.

    Sub. Major Lachman Singh, Bahadur, I.D.S.M.

Military Cross

    Capt. R. A. P. Grant (112th Inf. attd. 67th)

Order of the White Eagle (Serbia) 5th Class with Swords.

    Bt. Lt. Col. N. Ogle D.S.O.

Order of British India, 2nd Class.

    Sub-Maj. Lachman Singh, Bahadur, I.D.S.M.
    Subadar Ghulam Khan.
    Subadar Rahmat Ali.

Indian Distinguished Service Medal

        Sub-Maj. Lachman Singh, Bahadur.
4142 Hav. Shera (113th Inf. attd. 67th)
2332 Sepoy Nur Khan.
1397 L/N Khoja Khan.
1005 Nk. Munsabdar.
99   Hav. Tirloka.
3033 Hav. Harbans. (112th Inf. attd. 67th)
     Sub. Sharif Khan.
     Sub. Ahmed Khan.
     Sub. Indar Singh.
347 Sepoy Shiv Chand (1/9th B.I. attd 67th)
933 Sepoy Mehr Din.
1164 Hav. Gauhar Ali.
898 Hav. Chartu.
132 Hav. Mahan Singh.
580 Hav. Kanshi Ram.
1087 Nk. Sadhu Singh.
     Jem. Ali Ahmed.
     Sub. Wariam Singh. (74th attd. 67th)
     Jem. Khem Singh.
90   Sepoy Allah Ditta.
741 Hav. Jazu Khan (2/67th).

Medal of the Order of St George (Russian), 2nd Class

1309 Nk. Feroze Khan.

Cross of the Order of Karageorge (Serbian), 1st Class, with swords

Sub. Piaru.

Serbian Silver Medal for Valour.

2041 L/N Dost Mahomed.
1683 Bugler Hardit Singh.

Meritorious Service Medal

     Jem. Shamas Din.
     Jem. Ram Singh.
     Jem. Hakam.
     Jem. Rahmat Khan.
1610 Hav. Fazal Khan.
2032 Hav. Mehr Khan.

1310 Hav. Karim Dad Khan.
727 Hav. Jodh Singh.
1087 Nk. Sadhu Singh.
682 Hav. Dalip Singh.
881 Hav. Fazal Khan.
355 Hav. Ishar Singh.
1577 Nk. Thakur Chand.

Mentioned in Despatches.

Lt. Col. W. R. B. Colan D.S.O. (3)
Bt. Lt. Col. C. E. S. Cox.
Bt. Lt. Col. N. Ogle (5)
Maj. H. N. Colan D.S.O. (2)
Maj. A. Riddell. D.S.O. (74th P.)
Maj. R. Bagnall. (74th P.)
Maj. R. F. Atkins.
Capt. M. C. Gribbon. (2)
Capt. R. A. P. Grant M.C. (112th Inf.)
Capt. T. Reed. (with 59th Rifles)
Capt. A. H. Crowther (2)
Capt. F. G. S. McLean.
2/Lt H. Arbuthnott (2)
Capt. G. C. Ballentine.
Capt. E. Curnow.
Capt. A. R. S. Hayne.
Capt. C. B. Sexton;
Capt. A. J. Hannah.
Lt. J. Murray.
Lt. H. B. Yorke.
Sub. Maj. Lachman Singh, Bahadur, I.D.S.M.(2)
Sub. Piaru.
Sub. Ghulam Khan, Bahadur.
Sub. Sharif Khan I.D.S.M.
Sub. Ahmad Khan I.D.S.M. (2)
Sub. Indar Singh I.D.S.M. (2)
Sub. Budh Singh.
Sub. Mahomed Din.
Sub. Wariam Singh (74th P.)
Jem. Ram Singh.
Jem. Totu Ram (2)
Jem. Hazure Singh.
Jem. Rahmat Khan.
Jem. Fazal Hassan.
Jem. Khem Singh.
Jem. Ali Ahmad I.D.S.M.
2613 L/N Feroze Khan (92nd P.)

4142 Hav. Shera I.D.S.M. (113th Inf.)
2332 Sepoy Nur Khan I.D.S.M. (2)
1005 Nk. Munsabdar I.D.S.M.
99   Hav. Tirloka I.D.S.M. (2)
1610 Hav. Fazal Khan.
1164 Hav. Gauhar Khan I.D.S.M. (2)
1941 Nk. Hadayat Khan.
1746 Hav. Ahmad Khan.
1471 Sepoy Gopal Singh.
1684 Hav. Gul Hassan.
1973 Hav. Jai Singh.
551 Hav. Jowala Singh (2)
1413 Hav. Kanshi Ram.
4973 Nk. Mehr Din.
1632 Hav. Shahbaz Khan (2)
90   Sepoy Alla Ditta
898 Hav. Chartu I.D.S.M.
1539 L/N Fazal Illahi
580 Hav. Kanshi Ram. I.D.S.M.
132 Hav. Mahan Singh I.D.S.M. (2)
933 Sepoy Mehr Din (2)
1087 Nk. Sadhu Singh I.D.S.M.
4192 Bugler Sher Shah (112th Inf.)
     Jem. Zulfi (74th P.)
169 Hav. Basant Singh (74th P.)
103 Hav. Lal Singh (2)
347 Sepoy Shiv Chand (1/9th B.I.)
1397 Nk. Khoja Khan.
2423 Sepoy Mahomed Zaman.
570 Hav. Dunna (69th P.)
1445 Hav. Fazal Khan (74th P.)
1649 Sepoy Fazal Dad.

APPENDIX G

Letter of Commendation

Extract from a letter from His Excellency the Commander-in-Chief in India to the Officer Commanding, Officers, and other Ranks of the 1/67th Punjabis on the Regiment's return from 5½ years' Active Service Overseas.

. . . . .

The record of your Services in Mesopotamia, in which country you took part in many actions, Salonica, Caucasus, Armenia and Anatolia, is one of which you may well be proud. Throughout the whole period the greatest determination and devotion to duty has been displayed by all ranks, and you have upheld the confidence and trust placed in you by your King-Emperor and Country.

. . . . .

www.ingramcontent.com/pod-product-compliance
Lightning Source LLC
Chambersburg PA
CBHW080903230426
43663CB00014B/2609